MEMOR  A

Una Hurst

ARTHUR H. STOCKWELL LTD.
Elms Court   Ilfracombe   Devon
Established 1898

© *Una Hurst, 1997*
First published in Great Britain, 1997
All rights reserved.
*No part of this publication may be reproduced
or transmitted in any form or by any means,
electronic or mechanical, including photocopy,
recording, or any information storage and
retrieval system, without permission
in writing from the copyright holder.*

*British Library Cataloguing-in-Publication Data.
A catalogue record for this book is available
from the British Library.*

ISBN 0 7223 3069-3

*Printed in Great Britain by
Arthur H. Stockwell Ltd.
Elms Court   Ilfracombe
Devon*

Memories of Africa

"Why did you go to Africa, Nan?" said my granddaughter one day.

It all happened so long ago, before she was born and I realised that she wanted to know all about it. "Well," I told her, "it was the very bad weather of 1947 . . ."

A sick baby, no coal for the whole of February, ice and snow outside, electricity off for large parts of the day; then came the news that industry would be without power. All these things built up to our decision to get away to the sunshine.

The idea of going to South Africa had been stored away at the back of our minds since 1931. At the age of twenty-one, after seven years' apprenticeship to the printing trade, my husband was without a job. He had no savings, as the wage for an apprentice in those days was only a few shillings a week, finishing up in his last year at twenty-five shillings.

About this time, a very old friend of my parents turned up out of the blue. He had left England at seventeen to go to South Africa with his family. Now, middle aged, with a wife and a grown-up daughter, this was his first trip back to England. My family had lost touch with him, but he eventually traced them through the local voters' roll.

We used to sit enthralled as he told us of his life in the Cape Province. He ran a general store selling all kinds of things to the natives. I remember him buying a consignment of cheap boots and various job lots of clothing to be sold in his shop when he returned. He took a liking to my husband and tried to persuade him to go back with him. He offered to lend him the cost of the sea passage, also the deposit which had to be made to the South African Government.

It was a wonderful opportunity and much heart-searching went on between us. I told him that I would not stand in his way and would go out to marry him as soon as he could afford it. At that time his father had just reached sixty-five and although most men worked much longer (the pension being only ten shillings a week) he had been made redundant due to the depression. To go abroad penniless did not appeal to my husband; he had his pride. It would take a long time to repay his debts before he could start saving. The plight of his family worried him. They had made sacrifices to keep him whilst he learned a trade. It would be a poor reward to go off now. He was confident that he would soon get work and paying his board would help his family. He turned down the offer with thanks. His optimism proved correct, after a few weeks he got work as a journeyman printer.

Our friend from South Africa was a man who liked to surprise people. He arrived unexpectedly in 1935 and again in 1938. We were married and in our own home and the question of emigrating never arose, although we always enjoyed hearing about South Africa. We received the occasional food parcels during the war and gifts at Christmas but then heard nothing more.

In February 1947, we became very despondent and we decided to write to South Africa enquiring about conditions there. We were saddened to hear that our friend had died but his widow wrote an encouraging letter, although we had never met her. We made numerous enquiries about the cost of living, housing, etc., and visited South Africa House. We sat up until the small hours discussing things. It was a decision that could not be made lightly. We decided on East London and my husband wrote to the mayor asking about local conditions. He replied saying that he also was a printer employed on the local newspaper and that they would be pleased to offer him a job.

The house and furniture were sold — a big wrench parting with so much that was dear to us. Shipping was expensive and we had to be drastic in cutting down to a minimum what we could afford to take with us. In those days not long after the war, it was difficult to get passages. We were advised by the 1820 Settlers Association that my husband should go first — obtain accommodation for the family, and have this duly certified by someone in authority. He flew out alone in September. I could smile now at the difference in air-travel. The first stop was Malta — no night flying — two more overnight stops before reaching Johannesburg. After another overnight stay, he travelled by train to East London. Weeks went by as I anxiously waited for the sailing tickets to arrive. We were staying with relatives and I assured the travel agents that I could go at very short notice if the opportunity arose. My memory of those last few weeks was washing the baby's clothes every day and drying the nappies in the oven, ready to pack. The tickets arrived in December and with butterflies in my stomach I set off on my long journey.

As the train steamed out on that dull December day, it really hit me that I was alone (or rather responsible for the children without any help). I wondered if I would ever see my family and friends again. Tears trickled down, but big boys don't cry and Philip was twelve. Mum had to set an example and I turned to look out of the window and swallowed the lump in my throat. There was no heating on the train and we huddled together for warmth. I had been told by the travel agents that the train had a dining car and looked forward to a hot dinner to see us through. There was no dining car, no buffet — nothing.

We arrived at Southampton in the dark and took our place in the queue for taxis. Eventually after a long wait we arrived at the hotel five minutes before the dining room closed. The hotel was very good indeed, but hardly what I had ordered in the circumstances. I had asked for a small quiet family hotel and there I was, walking across the reception area, ankle deep in carpet. The head waiter in tails stood by taking down our order for dinner, to be served in our room, as I wheeled baby along in her pushchair with her potty wrapped in brown paper, tied to the handle.

The following day I had to go to the station and remove the luggage labels and put the shipping ones on in their place. Walking across the booking hall with its wooden floor apparently hollow underneath, there was a plop and off fell the brown paper parcel with the potty. Philip was horrified and in a stage whisper said "Leave it Mum, everybody will know what it is." Oh the embarrassment of youth. Naturally after bringing it so far and knowing that she would refuse a new one, I picked it up and tied it on (more firmly this time).

We went abroad in the afternoon after passing through immigration and customs. It all seemed very noisy and confusing to me and I was shown to my cabin. My cabin, indeed; there were twelve of us, two tiers of bunks which just fitted in from door to wall and up to the one washbasin. We were allowed one suitcase to be kept under the bunk. Philip being twelve, was in with the men; so down we went to what seemed the bottom of the ship. He was in a dormitory with at a guess about fifty men. I was dismayed. What if he was ill? I could not go in there obviously. However, people are kind and although I had not spoken a word, they must have sensed my anxiety as several of the men told me not to worry, they would see that he was alright. Apparently all the passengers were not on board — the Midlands and the South that day and Scotland and the North the following day. I had a night to get adjusted, the seasick pills could wait until the next day. The bunks were not allocated and I was advised to take two lower ones at angles to one another. In this way it was easy for me to reach out to baby. This was just as well as circumstances proved. I had been told that if a cot was not available, the bunk would be netted or boarded. I asked the stewardess for the bunk to be made safe but was told that nothing could be done until the ship sailed and the stores made available. Sylvia fell out of her bunk and I caught her. From being fast asleep one moment, I was clutching arms and legs the next. I put her in my bunk next to the wall for the rest of the night. When I told the stewardess what had happened, a board was found and I had no further trouble for the rest of the voyage.

It was a thrill exploring the ship with its lounges, library and dining room. Although there were so many passengers (just under fifteen hundred I was told) one advantage was that the whole of the deck space was available — no barriers for first-class passengers only. When the ship was due to sail the following day, we had found our way around and were interested in watching the last-minute telegrams and bouquets of flowers arriving. Friends and relatives were standing waving a last farewell as the ship sailed slowly out to the strains of "Now is the hour when we must say farewell". It was a sad and touching moment. I shall always remember as I stood on deck in the cold fading light watching the last bit of England disappear.

Shortly after this, we were all summond to a boat drill; nicely timed to take our minds off things. We were shown how to don our life jackets and where to report if things went wrong. Best not dwell on that I thought, as I could not swim a stroke. As the boat was so full, we had two sittings for meals. There was no nursery or separate arrangements for young children. Meal times would see me struggling down the stairs with a child on one arm and a pillow clutched under the other, otherwise she would never have reached the table.

It was an unusual sensation going to sleep in a room with so many strangers, but the atmosphere was very friendly. Sylvia was the youngest but slept through the nights without any trouble. It was also strange to wake up in the morning and see a couple of feet dangling before my eyes as the lady above me descended. All kinds of entertainments were arranged; a baby show, a fancy dress for the children and one for adults. The ladies in our cabin persuaded me to enter Sylvia in the fancy-dress parade. We made her a grass skirt from green crepe paper with garlands of multi-coloured flowers threaded and hung round her neck and I pinned flowers in her hair. She looked very attractive but rather spoilt her chances when she took fright at parading around the deck and I had to carry her. They were all given an apple and an orange, and she streaked off along the deck. I heard a voice say "Just look at that kiddie" and a whirring of a cine camera. Someone, somewhere, has a shot of a very tiny South Sea maiden.

The green crepe paper came from the barber's shop; it was a popular place and seemed to have everything. I was amazed to see fifty English cigarettes for two shillings and twopence, and sweets and chocolate galore. The days passed pleasantly, first an early-morning walk round the deck with baby in her pushchair; after breakfast a trip to the washroom to do the daily washing and ironing, and the rest of the day lazing in a deck chair. The sea was calm and none of us were seasick. The weather gradually got warmer as we neared our only port of call, Las Palmas. It seemed strange to discard my woollens in December and wear a cotton dress, and bare legs with the remains of chilblains on my heels, did not seem quite right.

We reached Las Palmas about breakfast time; stalls were quickly set up on deck. The first things to catch my eye were the large Walkie-Talkie dolls. All along the quayside were pedlars wearing black berets mingling with the crowd. We were constantly stopped by men selling fancy jewellery, baskets of fruit, vases and genuine "Parker Pens". One passenger bought a pen and later discovered that it was an empty case. Cigarettes were more popular than cash; most of us had been told of this and went ashore with several boxes. The town itself was a mile or so away; taxis were honking and making a terrific din, but as we were only staying for two hours, I did not risk going further afield. I was afraid of being left behind.

We 'crossed the line' on Christmas Eve. I had heard a lot about ceremonies for this and felt rather let down as nothing was done apart from the announcement on the Tannoy. It seemed a very strange Christmas to me, perspiration rolling down my face as I listened to the familiar Christmas carols being relayed. Many were dressed for dancing; perfume and pretty dresses were around me, but after doing baby's washing, I went off to bed. Christmas can be a lonely time even in a crowd. Christmas Day was much better. The dining room was decorated and we had a very good dinner. Some of the stewards had overindulged; ice cream coming before the turkey at some tables, which raised a few smiles. No-one fell flat on their face and our steward was quite sober. After dinner we had an enjoyable ship's concert. The amount of real talent on board was surprising. We had been spared the willing but unqualified. The previous day we were sitting on the upper deck and overheard some of the rehearsals. Someone was attempting "You always hurt the one you love" and a passenger remarked that it was painful to us too. Most evenings there was dancing, dog racing films or Tombola, as we moved from midwinter to midsummer. Our winter clothes were packed away; the suitcases closed as I eagerly awaited my first glimpse of Cape Town. I was too excited to sleep much and four o'clock found me out on deck. The ship was anchored in Table Bay and shortly after this we sailed slowly into the harbour. The lights were twinkling on the distant shore and gradually as we drew near the sun came up. Towering into the skyline was Table Mountain and its sister mountains, the top covered in its mist "tablecloth", a most beautiful and awe-inspiring sight. After that we were back to the mundane things of life. All was bustle as immigration and customs officials came on board and we were interviewed. Money was exchanged for South African currency and at last I was told that I could go ashore. I waited for a long time at the top of the gangway for a porter, while experienced travellers clicked their fingers, called "boy" and were soon fixed up. Frankly I was scared stiff at the sight of these porters; eventually I gingerly held up my hand and one came forward to help me.

I thought Southampton was noisy but this was really daunting. Nearly fifteen hundred passengers were all trying to get away as quickly as possible. The heat was terrific; I was jostled aside every few minutes by porters with trolleys. However, rescue was at hand in the form of a Red Cross volunteer who offered to look after the baby for me. They also gave me tea and cake and after that I felt a little more prepared for the fray. I had one sticky moment when I reached the bench where the cases were checked. A most unpleasant official chalked a cross on my case but insisted on opening Philip's. Imagine a boy of twelve cramming all his things into a case; he could not even fasten it until an obliging passenger sat on it. They would choose that one I thought and explained that it only held clothes and toys — but no — it must be opened. Dirty socks, dominoes, games, etc., were all inspected and queried; small metal pieces similar to Meccano had to be accounted for, whilst I stood by holding, by that time, a crying child in my arms. He grudgingly chalked the case but I said I could not close it. With crowds waiting behind, he eventually managed to fasten it, going almost purple in the face with the effort. There were other queues to pass through before we could leave the docks and my Red Cross friend suggested that she took us to the Overseas Visitors' Club for lunch and I could return later in the afternoon when the crowds had left.

Naturally I was all agog to see Cape Town. My first impression was very much like America as I had seen it on the films. Wide streets, brilliant sunshine and large American cars everywhere. After lunch, I took a taxi to the docks and was soon passed through with the luggage. I took another taxi and left the luggage at the other station, where we were to catch the train in the evening. I found the post office and sent a telegram to my husband giving our time of arrival in East London. The post office was large, clean and airy; close by were the flower sellers with all kinds of exotic blooms for sale. It was fascinating, but just as I was thinking of getting a taxi back to the club, the awful thought struck me. I had forgotten the name of the place and the address. I dashed back to the post office, found a telephone directory and thought of all the names it might be. Luckily for me I found it. After that, I could not get back quick enough. I have heard about people going on holiday, leaving their luggage and going out for a stroll. Believe me it can happen.

We had tea at the club and then walked around the shops. After years of rationing and austerity, I could now show Philip the toys galore; wristwatches and cameras, everything to delight a schoolboy. It saddened me that he had missed so much through the war; we cannot put the clock back and he had outgrown many of them without experiencing the pleasure. After dinner at the club, we collected our light luggage and went off in yet another taxi to the station. It was New Year's Eve and there was a great deal of laughing and shouting in the streets and many were decidedly drunk. One coloured man, fighting with a stick, stumbled in front of our taxi and was nearly knocked down. I was relieved when we reached the station and sat on the platform waiting for the train. It was then quite dark; everything seemed very strange and I was very tired. When the train pulled in, my Red Cross friend of the morning, appeared to see us safely onto the train. This act of kindness from a stranger, touched me very much, especially as New Year's parties were in full swing. Once on our way, the bedding steward came to make up the beds in our compartment, and after a tiring and exciting first day in South Africa, we were thankful to stretch ourselves out and sleep.

The next morning, we were awakened by a tapping on the door and were served with large cups of coffee. Up went the blinds; now for another look at our new country — nothing but the red soil and prickly bush of the Karoo. All the wayside halts and stations were most interesting to me with the natives playing their banjos and the piccanins running alongside the train for sweets and pennies.

In the middle of the afternoon, we had to change trains at a small station with not a house in sight. On the platform was a notice board with the names of the passengers and compartment numbers. Everyone had to book in advance because of sleeping arrangements. Our names were not down on the board, although I had booked through to East London. Up and down the platform I went looking for an inspector but all I could find were busy porters who did not understand my English or did not wish to do so. Many of the railway employees were Afrikaners. Meanwhile everyone else was safely on board. Luckily for me, two young men jumped off the train and said they could not leave me there. They found an inspector and an empty coach was hitched onto the train, and once more we were on our way.

At daybreak I was delighted to see pleasant green countryside; we had left the Karoo behind and were getting near to the end of our journey. At every station we were out in the corridor absorbing the atmosphere of it all. I saw some native women with black silk-fringed shawls and black silk squares on their heads and long dark spotted dresses. A lady passenger told me that this type of dress denoted great respectability. I was now familiar with the women, bundles of all shapes on their heads, carrying their babies on their backs tied on with a shawl. I have always preferred to keep an eye on my children and wondered if this was the origin of the expression "eyes in the back of your head"? They certainly needed them there.

At last we reached East London — there was my husband waiting on the platform. Would baby remember him or would she cry? One quizzical little look she gave, then off she went holding Daddy's hand to supervise the luggage being put into the car. I had a pleasant surprise as my husband had bought a car; a second-hand Plymouth. It seemed huge to me after our little nine horsepower back home. Now we were mobile and ready to explore our new country.

I found East London a most attractive resort with its lovely coastline, silvery sands, and everywhere the line of white surf as the sea broke on the rocks. It was however very breezy when sitting on the open beach. The main streets were wider than my home town of Leicester, with streams of large cars and the traffic policemen in khaki uniforms racing along on motorcycles or in police vans. I found it rather disconcerting as they broadcast rude comments on the standard of drivers; far removed from our friendly "bobbies".

When we arrived, the Centenary celebrations were on and the main streets were a mass of fairy lights, with the town hall floodlit. It was a pleasure to go out at night after so many years of blackout and dim-out. Most of the houses were single storey, with cream washed walls and corrugated roofs painted red or green, and standing in large gardens. For the first week we drove out to various local beauty spots, taking a primus stove and frying pan and having a picnic lunch South African style.

My husband returned to work; Philip started at his new school and I must confess I felt rather lost. We had furnished rooms in a large house standing well back from the road on a double plot. The accommodation was good, but the owners of the house with whom we shared, went away the day after we arrived. I was left to cope with a native servant girl named Doris. She spoke practically no English and I came up against the language problem with no-one to advise me. If she had forgotten to clean under the beds, or I wanted the kitchen floor scrubbed, I was reduced to waving my arms about like a windmill in action. She burnt a large hole in my best nightdress; I found it neatly ironed and folded with the exact shape of the iron missing.

When I went out to the shops, young native girls came up to me saying "You want nurse girl missis —?" I did not want a nurse girl but apparently most people had one. I went in the park one day and did not see a white woman there at all. Little groups of native nurse girls sat chatting on the grass, while their white charges played around. Obviously I could not find friends there. Apparently it was not the done thing to push one's own pram around. I felt lonely on my own all day with practically nothing to do except cook a meal.

My landlady wrote and asked me to take the house girl along to clean out one of their houses that they let furnished to people on holiday. The lady who lived next door saw me and asked me inside, followed by an invitation to go to tea. Whilst having tea with her and her friends, they casually mentioned Samp. "What is Samp?" I asked and was told that it was the main food for the servants. A kind of dried mealies and beans; it was cooked for hours and meat and vegetables added. When I told them that I had never heard of it, they asked me what I gave the girl for her meals. I said that she had the same as us; bacon and eggs for breakfast, meat and vegetables and fruit and cream for the main meal. They were shattered. What an embarrassing moment it was for me, but how was I to know, no-one had told me otherwise? I went to the hairdressers one day. When I offered her a tip, she explained that I must never give tips to South African hairdressers, cafes or anywhere; it was not done.

When the landlord and his wife returned, I found things rather difficult. Water was metered and he told me that when I washed my hands I must leave the dirty water in the washbowl and not waste it. I was disgusted, what a filthy habit and yet it was a very nice house in a good-class neighbourhood. I received constant warnings about not allowing baby to drop crumbs on the carpets as they were very valuable. Our dining-cum-sitting room had a wardrobe containing their things and it was kept locked. Practically every time I put a meal on the table, she came in with the excuse that she wanted something out of the wardrobe and we had almost no privacy. I put the bone from our Sunday joint in the kitchen waste bin one day. Later that morning, I noticed a pan on the stove boiling over. Lifting the lid, I saw our discarded bone cooking away with vegetables. When I said I had switched the hotplate down for her, she told me that the bone was too good to throw away and she had taken it for their lunch.

We managed to get two unfurnished rooms with a small furnished bedroom for Philip, and shared the kitchen. The house was in a pleasant district but we jumped out of the frying pan into the fire. We bought furniture for the bedroom and lounge/dining room and my own pots and pans.

The arrangements for washing clothes were very primitive. I had to buy a washboard (I had never seen one before, not even in my childhood) and a large galvanised bath. The wash girl arrived on Monday or Tuesday morning; the bath taken outside, filled with warm water and with only a piece of ordinary washing soap, rubbed away at the clothes. Underclothes in particular wore out very quickly; in fact when I arrived, my husband's had large holes in them after three months' wear. The house girl was shared. The landlady fed her and I paid her wages. I did not need a girl for cleaning a few rooms but had no choice in the matter. Folks got up early and the girl cleaned the other part of the house between six-thirty and seven o'clock. She had her breakfast and came to me. All the furniture was piled into the centre of the room, the carpet turned up at the edges and then — a shrill voice called out "Annie". That was the last I saw of her for at least an hour. What a muddle I was in until she eventually returned. When I complained to the landlady and said I preferred to wait, I was told it was her servant and she could have her when she wanted. This performance went on every day. The garden was only a small piece of grass with a border around. One day Sylvia stood on the grass to speak to a little boy next door. Knock knock on the window "Bring that child in, she will ruin my garden" and she had not touched a thing. I wondered why people let rooms to children if they dislike them so much. I took her out in the pushchair; she had nowhere to play and never got dirty. Every Saturday we went into town shopping. The shops all closed at lunch time for the weekend, so it had to be in the morning. Apparently I was doing wrong again as the landlady told me that I was in South Africa now (her favourite opening gambit) and women did not go shopping with their husbands, they stayed at home and cooked the lunch. I quietly told her, that was strange, as the town was full of families out shopping together and that my husband liked me to go out with him. I would put the bacon on for breakfast and as soon as I went out of the kitchen to set the table, she took the pan off. Why this was I never found out as the arrangement was for me to have two of the four hotplates, and I always kept carefully to my side. I was allowed to use the oven only on Sundays, except if she baked in the week, then she allowed me to put something of mine in the oven; so cooking was becoming quite a problem. It is not easy to make friends when one is living in rooms. As a householder one is more established, but in a seaside resort such as East London with its changing population of holiday-makers I made few friends. Family life as I had always known it, seemed nonexistent. Morning and afternoon tea parties were popular but the children were not there. They were either left at home with the nurse girl or played together in the garden with a girl or two in charge. Any refreshments they had, were given to them in the kitchen or the garden, never in the house with the mothers. It was quite a common sight to see a native girl walking along the street with a small European child on her back. I have seen them sitting on the kerbstone, while the child played in the gutter; the nurse girl taking an occasional swig at the child's bottle.

The newspapers arrived about four in the morning, and we were out looking for other rooms before six o'clock. It was a miserable time and I often longed to be back in England. It was about this time that we experienced heavy floods. It started to rain as we went for a short drive on the Sunday afternoon. It was like a cloudburst with rain pouring down the deep gutters. We sat in the car for a while and then made a dash for inside. All that night, all the next day, and on to the Tuesday, the rain thundered down on the corrugated roof; it was deafening. When the rain stopped, we went out to see the extent of the damage as stories had come in of cattle being washed away, trees uprooted, the swollen rivers carrying everything before it down to the sea. We found Nahoon Beach completely altered. The lovely high sand dunes had gone, leaving a flat beach; the children's swings in their concrete bases, had been washed away into the sea. It looked as though the whole area had been bulldozed. Nature can be very terrifying.

At Las Palmas, I had bought one of those lovely Walkie-Talkie dolls for Sylvia; although she was rather young for it, I could not resist them. One day she was playing with it and the arm came off. My husband tried to mend it without success, and of course there were tears. I remembered seeing an advertisement in the local paper for a doll's hospital. I rang the number and was given a time to call. Dolly was carefully wrapped in a shawl and off we went. We were greeted by the 'doctor' in a white coat. We all sat down in his room and the doll was solemnly examined. He told Sylvia that her baby was very sick and would have to stay in his hospital, but he could make her better. Wide-eyed she agreed to leave her doll and we had to call back in a week's time. Sure enough, there was the doll skilfully mended; a wonderful chance to give her confidence in doctors and hospitals.

We had been looking round for a place of our own and bought a plot in the suburbs overlooking the Buffalo river. It was a different proposition to buying a house in England. There were no housing estates to choose from. We had plans drawn up and passed by the local authorities and were approved for a mortgage. There were no roads but had been told that when most of the houses were built in the township as it was called, we could ask the authorities to build the roads; we should be charged for this work when it was completed. There were no sewers and we arranged for a septic tank to be installed. We found a builder who had built his own house nearby and was prepared to do the work for us. In the meantime we took two unfurnished rooms in a house overlooking our plot, and waited for our house to go up. First the deeds of the land went missing somewhere between the agents and the solicitors. They searched everywhere and it meant a delay of several weeks. Apparently they had to advertise in the press, and if they did not turn up after a certain time, copies had to be made. They assured us that in all their experience such a thing had never happened before — well it happened to us. Snag number two was when the builder came round to tell us that he had to go into hospital and could not do the work for us. We tried and tried to find another builder at a price we could afford, but there was a shortage of cement, and prices had rocketed. We sat up until the early hours of the morning revising the plans of the house, cutting out the garage, cutting out the servant's quarters, etc., and still had no quote that we could afford. When I remembered my pleasant house and garden back in England, I could have wept, but tears would not build us a house. We thought perhaps we would do better to look elsewhere for a home, we had encountered so many difficulties. My husband heard of a job in King William's Town, about thirty-seven miles inland. They were offering a house to rent. He applied and we drove over to look at the place. The house was old but roomy; at last we had found a home.

The move however could hardly be called smooth by any stretch of imagination. The children and I had picked up a tummy bug and were laid up before the move. We felt pretty groggy when the van arrived at six-thirty in the morning. After loading the special items and radio into the car, we set out to collect two black kittens and one white rabbit. It probably sounded rather crazy but we felt the children deserved pets after being cooped up in other folks' houses for so long. One kitten jumped out of my arms as we walked to the car and after a wild scramble it was caught and we set out. Halfway along the journey, the car started making ominous noises and came to a halt. We did get to King William's Town, but not together. I waited for the removal van to come along and climbed aboard with baby, leaving the two males to wait for a tow. What a start in a new town. We all met up at the house around noon; the shops closed at one o'clock for the weekend and we dashed to the shops to collect some food to tide us over the Saturday and Sunday.

Native girls soon came round asking for work and this was my first experience of choosing a servant. I took one on and hoped for the best. The servant's room was in the garden. We had to supply her with a bed, eating utensils, cap and apron and give her food. Mildred was a good worker and a great help at the time as I was feeling very ill. I struggled on for several days and decided I must see a doctor. It was a worrying time; there I was in a strange town not knowing a soul and ordered to stay in bed with the prospect of being sent to hospital if I did not improve within a few days. My illness turned out to be a blessing in disguise. The first evening, a visitor called from the Sons of England Association. He was very concerned, brought his wife around, told the vicar and I received callers ready to help. Luckily I did not need to go into hospital and by the time I was up and about, had gained several friends.

One afternoon about five o'clock, I was in the garden, and my husband told me I had visitors. Two ladies from nearby had 'called'. They apologised profusely for not bringing a visiting card; they had run out of them. I assured them that it was not important but they seemed worried at not conforming to their usual standard. Apparently a first call should be made between tea and dinner; no refreshments taken, but a visiting card presented. They were two very kind old ladies, still clinging to past tradition that had died out in England long ago. The mayoress gave an At Home about once a month and anyone who was invited made a point of reading Caroline's gossip column, to see if they were mentioned. I was invited soon after my arrival and bought a new hat for the occasion. My name appeared in the next issue as welcoming a newcomer to the town. The shop assistants were very obliging; goods would be taken home on approval and returned. Every purchase was followed by "Must I enter it?" No-one seemed to pay cash. A newcomer from England went to pay his monthly account and was asked how much he wanted to pay, and assured that it was not necessary to pay in full. Friends showed me dresses they had bought months before and still owed for them. One young man laughingly told us that he had just bought a new American car and had no cash to tax it. He told them to add it to the account. Debts did not seem to worry South Africans.

King William's Town was a pleasant little place, laid out on English lines, with its main street, town hall and market square. It had a good public library, a museum, post office and police station (they called it the charge office). I had always enjoyed Leicester Market and the neighbours told me that the market in 'King' was the best place to shop for fresh fruit, vegetables and various other things. A leisurely afternoon visit was not possible, as the market closed before noon. At about six-thirty, I used to set out down the street (we lived in Market Street), with a huge straw basket over my arm. The market square was already bathed in brilliant sunshine. There were no stalls. Everything was laid out in 'lots' on the ground. Trays of tomatoes, oranges, rows of pumpkins, pineapples and cabbages were lined up like a regiment of soldiers. Folks stood around waiting for the auctioneer to arrive. A box-like contraption on wheels with a canopy, rather like a Punch and Judy outfit was wheeled up; in stepped the auctioneer and the gabbling started. If I did not speak up or lift my hand, the stuff was gone. I felt like a non-swimmer thrown in at the deep end. Standing there alone on my first visit, a voice behind me said "You are new here aren't you?" and I was told how to bid and what to look for. We moved down the market as the goods were sold; eggs and poultry came next. The auctioneer stepped out of his box and we all trooped after him to the inside market. Here there were heaps of peas and beans, carrots in bundles and heaps of potatoes and sweet potatoes. Finally came the flowers — gorgeous scented carnations, masses of larkspur and other flowers. While all this was going on, small African boys were standing against the wall outside waiting for a job. To a snapping of fingers and a cry of 'piccanin' one of them dashed up and I walked home; the piccanin following behind with the basket on his head. I enjoyed going to market; I met folks and often shared a tray of fruit or tomatoes, if it was a large one. Native girls, who also bought at the market, often called at the house. They used to walk up the garden path to the back veranda with either a large box or a mysterious bundle on their head. These would be laid out on the ground for inspection. Another way for them to earn money was to go round the houses on a Monday or Tuesday to do the weekly wash. At about eight o'clock she would arrive complete with baby on her back and a small girl. While the mother worked, the little girl sat in the garden and kept the baby amused. It was usual to give them breakfast about ten, consisting of mealie meal porridge, bread and jam or treacle, and a large mug of tea. For the main meal of the day, they had a dish piled high with stamped mealies and beans with meat and vegetables. Now and again we had the 'Red Blanket Kaffirs' around, usually selling brooms. They dressed in an orange-coloured blanket draped round the body, leaving the shoulders bare, the hem stamped with a dark brown pattern. Round their arms and ankles they wore numerous bracelets that jangled as they walked along. Their faces were covered in a kind of white clay or sometimes yellow ochre. They looked a weird crowd as they walked around the town chattering and laughing among themselves. On Saturday and Sunday afternoons, we often saw them in the open country dancing and clapping their hands as the cars passed. We went for a drive near the Lovedale University, a modern college for natives. On the way we saw kraals with pigs and chickens and children all together in very primitive conditions in their mud huts. Then again, in East London, I often saw native girls shopping in the better-class shops; extremely well dressed, high-heeled shoes and faces skilfully made-up; truly a land of contrasts. The colour bar was strict and in some cases confusing. We had a sticky moment on the bus one day. My pipe-smoking husband naturally made for the stairs to the upper deck. Seeing a notice, that natives only were allowed on top, I quickly called out to him to come back. Sometimes they were allowed at the front inside. One did not mix; trying to break the colour bar, would get anyone into trouble. Shopping in the suburbs, there would probably be half a dozen natives waiting to be served, but the moment I walked in, the shopkeeper served me. I did not like it, but what could one do in these circumstances? Our local cinema had one row at the back for natives; a partition separating them from the Europeans. Some cinemas did not allow them in at all. At the printing works, natives did the labouring; they were not allowed to learn skilled jobs.

    Our first Christmas in South Africa was very different from back in England; being midsummer it was very hot. I went into East

London with a friend to do my Christmas shopping and sat on the beach to cool off — no snow — no frost. We had the usual Christmas dinner of turkey and plum pudding and mince pies; not the ideal fare, but everyone had it. On Christmas morning piccanins came round to the door smiling and saying "Christmas"; we handed out pennies until we saw a procession of at least a dozen and decided that it was time to call a halt.

Life in a small community is much the same the world over. I was soon helping with the church bazaar, attending various women's meetings and selling flags on street corners on Saturday mornings. I felt that this was not enough to occupy my days. I had always been active and decided to become a corsetière. I went to East London for a short training course, returning home each evening. We were told to practise fitting a modelling garment on a friend or relative. I had no relatives and did not know anyone well enough to ask them to strip off for a fitting. My husband was a good sport and with a cushion round his middle and with much laughter between us, I laced him into the modelling garment. It was quite a new venture for me and I thoroughly enjoyed meeting new people.

One day, we drove to Grahamstown to deliver a corset and stopped halfway at a general store, and asked them to display my showcard. Shortly after this I had a phone call asking me to go over as several ladies were interested. It was a small farming community called Peddie, and how to get there was a problem, as I did not drive. I discovered that the railway bus ran there and booked a ticket. The front compartment was high up (first class) with padded seats, similar to a railway carriage. At the rear were numerous native passengers and bags of produce to be delivered to the outlying farms. The goods were delivered, pleasantries exchanged and off we went again. Once there was shouting from the back of the bus; the driver pulled up and out dashed a number of native men to relieve themselves in the bushes; it was back to nature out there.

I had lunch at the one hotel and gave one lady a fitting in her bedroom. She then took me over to the village hall. The ladies met once a month, as it was a very scattered community. I was made very welcome, given tea and cake when, to my utter dismay, the chairman rang a little bell and announced that I would give a talk on corsetry. That is one way to start public speaking, to be thrust into it without warning, but I had to do something. I explained that it was usual to give a private fitting and rather difficult without a model. That did not let me out, one lady immediately offered to oblige, stripped down in an adjoining room and the demonstration went ahead. I took several orders on the spot.

Now that I was working, I depended more on my servant girl and I came up against trouble for the first time. It was usual for them to have the afternoon off and return in time to prepare the evening meal. Once or twice I had suspected Mildred of being slightly tipsy as she teetered across the garden swinging her scarf in the air, but she had done her work and I thought it best to ignore it. We awoke on the first of the month to find that she had disappeared overnight. This was a common occurrence, as they were paid on the last day of the month, and often decided to move on without telling anyone. In this case, however, all her clothes were still in her room. I rang the hospital and charge office fearing that she had met with an accident or been locked up, but no-one had seen her. Later that day a neighbour's girl said Mildred had been seen in the location sleeping off a drunken bout. Her room was rather grubby and I dropped her caps and aprons into a bucket of water with plenty of soap powder and Dettol and left them on the stove to boil. Rinsing them out I felt something soggy in the pocket and drew out two one-pound notes. I dried them out and they seemed none the worse — the cleanest notes in Africa.

Word soon went round when a servant was needed and about six-thirty the following morning a young native girl was waiting on the back veranda. "What is your name?" I asked. A smile lit up her face as she bobbed a quick half curtsy. "Vera, missis" she said. The faded cotton dress, clean and pressed, clung to her sturdy young figure, outlining the full young breasts. Around her wrists and ankles were a number of coloured bracelets; a gay blue nylon scarf was knotted at the back of her head, the ends fluttering behind her. She appeared to be about sixteen. In a short time, the servant's room had been swept and scrubbed; the clothes of her predecessor packed in a cardboard box awaiting her return. After a few days, her shyness wore off a little, and she told me of her boyfriend who worked far away in Cape Town. She had been educated at a mission school near her village. She wrote her love letters in a neat hand and received bulky letters in return. In the afternoon, she would sit in the shade outside her room, embroidering sheets and pillowcases ready for the day when she would be married. Her boyfriend had given her father fourteen cows and was working to buy six more. Her parents had sent her to the town to work to provide the cooking pots for her new home. In addition, she was to be fitted out with the dark blue and white spotted dresses, reaching down to her ankles, with head squares to match. She would also have a black-fringed shawl.

Vera was of a happy disposition, singing softly as she worked in the garden, bending over the big galvanised bath and rubbing the clothes on the wooden washboard. One morning, I was preparing the lunch, when an old native woman walked up the garden path. She bobbed and smiled and burst into a stream of conversation. I could not understand a word of it and called Vera to find what it was about. They greeted one another with handshakes, smiles and shouts of laughter. This was her auntie she told me who had come to measure her for the new dresses. "Could she go off to her room for a little while?" For the rest of the day she entertained me with details of the trousseau. Auntie was going back to the village and she and the girl's mother would set to work making the new clothes. Vera seemed so young to be married and appeared little older than my own children.

One morning, I was waiting in the post office as two young native men walked in; so different from the locals. It was obvious they were from one of the big cities. Brown and white pointed shoes, bright socks, neatly pressed trousers, smart tweed jackets, white shirts and brilliant ties, were topped by wide-brimmed felt hats. One carried a guitar; the other a portable gramophone. They were soon the centre of an admiring group. Returning home, I thought no more of it until, a little later, glancing out of the window, to my surprise, the same two young men were walking through the garden. What excitement for Vera; here was the boyfriend all the way from Cape Town, she told me. Every afternoon the garden resounded to the music from the gramophone. Unfortunately there was trouble in store. Luke was cross. He had left her safely at home in the village, now they had sent her to the town to work. "No good would come of it" he said. "There were wicked people in the towns and one would become a bad woman." Vera assured him that she would not go out, but still he was not satisfied.

The time drew near for his return to Cape Town. It was a beautiful soft evening; the sky full of stars. All was still, the hooter had already sounded warning the natives to be off the streets. All the servants were expected to be indoors, even if they were married; their husbands were not allowed to remain with them in their quarters.

That was the law, anyone caught offending, was quickly taken away to the charge office. Suddenly the silence was broken by hearty male laughter coming from Vera's room. We were horrified, that must be Luke in her room. My husband went over and told him to be out double quick, before he was caught. A downcast young man walked slowly to the gate followed by Vera. Her white apron glinted in the moonlight as she disappeared through the gate after him. Then, we were really worried; two of them out in the street after curfew. We waited anxiously as the minutes ticked by and decided to put out the lights and watch. Within a short time, they both tiptoed across the lawn into her room. The police could and did make spot checks at any time. In a very firm but whispered conversation, he was told he must go or there would be trouble for all of us.

The following morning, I had to tackle her. What could I say, confronted with the wide-eyed look of innocence on her face? "What would happen if he gave you a baby?" I asked. "Oh no missis" she said. "I would not get a baby." I wondered just how much she knew of the facts of life. Luke was not happy at waiting so long. Six more cows cost a lot of money.

He borrowed a bicycle and rode off to her village about forty miles away, to plead with her parents to reduce the number of cows. The hours dragged by as Vera went about her duties with downcast eyes. Late in the afternoon, a hot and perspiring native boy returned and they disappeared into her room. He had been told that times were bad. This was the year of the drought; the crops had failed. Two of the cows had already died. Vera was his only remaining daughter; the marriage payment was to help keep his wife and himself for the rest of their days. The dresses were not ready; there was not sufficient money for the cooking pots. He, a respected young man of his tribe, could not allow his daughter to be given in marriage without paying his share of the bargain. The following day, Luke set off on the bus to visit his own family. When he returned, a tearful Vera told us that she must leave us to go and live with his people until he had saved sufficient money for the cows. They would look after her until the marriage. She did not want to leave us, but there was nothing that I could do — other countries — other customs and one must respect them.

Shortly after we arrived in King William's Town, the spring rains were much less than usual, but as I knew little about the seasons, I paid no attention, especially after the floods of the previous year. I did not realise that during the winter, very little rain fell. After a time, water restrictions came into force. As the position grew worse, water was turned off during the night. When it was turned on again, it was a dark rusty colour and lots had to be run off before it was usable for anything. Gradually the hours for 'water on' were shortened until we only had water available from noon until two in the afternoon. It was difficult to make a native girl understand that every drop was precious, and that she must no longer wash her hands and feet under the garden tap, walking off to leave the water running as they were in the habit of doing.

We had made a pleasant little garden and lawn but nothing was green any more. All we had was brown dust, and each time the wind blew, the top soil went with it. Conditions had altered very much politically since we arrived. The residential qualifications for voting had been extended from two to five years for newcomers, and it was not certain that we would get the vote even then. There was no National Health Scheme as we had known. We had our share of sickness as any family does. When anyone was ill, there was a doctor's bill and a chemist's to meet. If Len fell ill, no money would come in at all. Fortunately none of us had to go into hospital, but there was always the nagging fear that if we were seriously ill, we would be faced with large bills from the hospital.

Chance plays a strange part in our lives. One day, I gave a fitting to a client who had recently arrived from Northern Rhodesia. Her husband had retired from a government post. She told me that conditions in service there included a furnished house and six months' leave overseas after three years, with passage paid. We called round to see them and heard that there was a Government Printing Department in Lusaka. Once again, we burned the midnight oil discussing our future. My husband wrote off enquiring about possible employment there. References and credentials were posted off and he was told that they would recommend him when a vacancy arose. We thought that probably nothing would happen for a long time, but it was worth applying. The thought of going back to England for a holiday was like a dream. Would it ever happen? A few weeks later we had a telegram from Lusaka offering employment. Could we be ready to go in four weeks' time? We wired back saying "YES". We called at the auctioneers and arranged for all our new furniture to be sold. Everything had to go with the exception of linen, carpets, etc. Once again we were pulling up our roots; smaller ones this time, but nevertheless I had been happy there and knew that I should miss the good friends that we had made. On the afternoon of the sale, the house was crowded, (auctions were popular in South Africa); everything was sold down to the few hens we kept in the garden and the rolls of netting. A friendly neighbour lent us beds for a few days. We stayed on at the house busily packing our remaining goods and chattels and went out for meals.

We decided to hold a farewell party to all our friends. All we had was a kitchen table; sold but not yet collected. We borrowed plenty of chairs and cushions. As a party it was great fun and quite a novelty in an empty house. Everyone turned up to give us a rousing farewell. For the last night we stayed in a local hotel. I crawled into bed, utterly exhausted and far too tired to worry or have any regrets. The next morning was all rush as we crammed our night things into the cases, handed over the keys of the house and drove off in a taxi to the station. Some of our friends were at the station and it was with mixed feelings that I said farewell to King William's Town.

Our train journey to the north was long and boring. It was not easy to keep a two-year-old and a twelve-year-old schoolboy amused for days on end, cooped up in our compartment. We had various stops, Kimberley (no diamonds in the gutter), Mafeking (long ago relieved). We had hours to wait at these places; dusty and drab. We walked along the main streets with ugly buildings and no places to interest us and back to the station to wait for yet another connection. The towns appeared to be smaller and more scattered as we travelled on.

Bulawayo was a pleasant surprise. After passing through immigration and customs, and changing our South African money into Rhodesian currency, we took a taxi to the town centre. The streets were wide and clean with blocks of modern shops. We had coffee in a pleasant cafe, filled with Saturday morning shoppers, and started to explore. Unfortunately all the shops closed at noon for the weekend and the town ground to a halt. Sitting in a small cafe for lunch, we were very surprised to hear most of the folks speaking in Afrikaans. Southern Rhodesia was a British colony; I had not realised that so many South Africans lived there. After lunch, we were in the same position as before; nowhere to go and nothing to do, not even the railway carriage to sit in. We had to wait until the evening for our train to arrive. Things began to liven up as several wedding parties arrived. The Victoria Falls was a popular place for honeymooners, and the station had a festive air with bridesmaids and well-dressed families waving them farewell.

Once more we were back in English-speaking territory, only English was spoken by the stewards on the trains. Yorkshire and Cockney accents made us feel at home. It was disappointing to have our first view of Victoria Falls from the train. We had heard so much about them, but the train passed slowly over the bridge without stopping and it was impossible to take in the wonders of it all, in those few seconds.

As we drew into Livingstone, the station was packed with natives with packages of all shapes and sizes, laughing and talking together. Immigration and customs officials interviewed us on the train as we travelled yet further north. The temperature was rising as we neared the tropics. The scenery did not vary much for the rest of the way; trees and bushes and still more bushes. We arrived in Lusaka in the dark on the Sunday evening. One of Len's new colleagues was waiting to meet us. We tried to sort out the luggage, but with no lights and no platform, we gave up looking for the heavier items and walked over to the hotel. The receptionist said "Oh, I thought you were coming tomorrow." What a welcome!! They found us one bedroom with six beds. They might have fetched a good price as antiques with deep hollows in the middle and bumps at the edges. We sorted out four of the best of them and unpacked. The one thought uppermost in my mind was to have a bath. For weeks we had been managing with a bowl of water and now we were free of water restrictions. How I enjoyed that bath and so into bed ready for a clean start in Northern Rhodesia.

The next day was a public holiday and we set out to explore the town. This did not take very long. There seemed to be only one main street with general dealers, drapers, a chemist and two hotels. The road was a narrow strip of tar down the centre; the sides, dirt and dust. All the buildings were on one side of the road; the other side, vacant grassland with the station in the rear. My first impression was a Wild West town, with swinging doors to the bar. I expected someone to be thrown out any minute. No-one rode up and tethered his horse to the pillars of the hotel, but the setting was there for a typical Western film. At a first inspection, many of the buildings one expects to see in a capital were missing. For instance where were the churches? After a time I found them dotted here and there; also a public open-air swimming pool, but there was no town hall. The large government offices stood out as a landmark about two miles from the town centre, referred to as the "Biscuit Factory".

The following day my husband started to work and I went along to arrange for Philip to start at his new school. I came up against a problem there, as the headmaster said it would be better for him to go back to Dale College in King William's Town as a boarder. All that way back again — and Philip refused point blank to go there. Until that time, the school had only catered for younger boys, but due to the increase in the population, they were gradually stepping it up, and a class for boys of his age was just starting, and he was enrolled. At lunch time I was told that we had been allocated a house and could move in the following morning. It was about four miles from the town; there were twenty-six houses; no shops. We were advised to order plenty of groceries and a load of wood for cooking on the wood-burning stove and for heating the water from an outside boiler. In a daze, I went into corner shops, opened monthly accounts and ordered the groceries. The firewood was ordered from an Indian drapery shop which seemed rather unusual.

Our house was in an attractive area aptly named Woodlands. The roads were named after the many trees that grew there.

Originally called Musase, Mubanga, etc., were soon changed to Ash, Birch, Cedar and Elm — much easier for us, though technically incorrect. The road from town, though narrow, was tarred until it reached the gates of Government House; after that, we rattled along a bumpy dirt road. Some of the houses were thatched, others had aluminium roofs and all were cream washed outside. All the windows had mosquito netting in addition to the glass, and the large shady veranda had only mosquito netting. The houses were classed as semi-permanent; presumably intended to last for only a few years. The rooms were large and airy; the kitchen very primitive with a cold-water tap, sink and wood-burning stove. We had three bedrooms and a bathroom. The water for the bath came from an outside wood-burning boiler. All the heavy furniture was supplied and checked off on a list. All the doors and cupboards had locks; we were handed a huge bunch of keys. Henceforth my husband used to say he clanked like Marley's ghost.

All our household equipment had travelled by goods train and did not arrive until six weeks later. Although we now had a home, it was a case of camping out, although neighbours were very kind and lent us lots of things. Apparently this was a common occurrence. The nights were chilly and in the dark evenings we sat by the fireside piling the dried seed pods onto the fire. These fell in profusion to the sounds of loud cracking on our aluminium roof and were useful for a quick cheerful fire.

An African turned up asking for work. Here it was the men who did the housework and cooking. I set him on as a general boy. The following day he produced two young boys, one to be houseboy, the other as garden-boy. My staff was now complete, and seemed a ridiculous number for a family of four. Apparently a cook did not wash the dishes and clean the house; a houseboy did not chop the wood and clean the shoes. When the firewood arrived, it was in huge logs and we had to buy a large axe for the garden-boy to cope with it. The cooking stove and the outside boiler used a considerable amount of wood. The garden-boy spent most of his time chopping and stacking it. Cooking by the old-fashioned stove was my biggest headache. It was difficult to adjust; when dry it burned too quickly, and when wet, too slowly. For the first few weeks I had more cooking failures than the rest of my life. My cakes were of the hit-and-miss variety. I found the heat in the kitchen very trying and reluctantly decided that I must leave it to the cook.

All the houses had cement floors to prevent the white ants eating through to the furniture; given a chance, they would destroy wood at an alarming rate. These floors looked attractive when well polished; ours were all red; others either black or green. The problem was making the staff understand that only a little polish was needed. I almost despaired, everywhere was red polish. It stuck to the soles of our shoes and transferred to the carpets. Sylvia's socks and dresses were covered in it from sitting on the floor. I decided to change to colourless wax polish and things improved.

The toilet outside the house was very primitive. Under the seat was a bucket and a trap door in the wall. Every evening at dusk, a figure crossed the garden, a pole slung over his shoulders, and at each end of the pole, a bucket. I had a shock once when the trap door opened and the bucket vanished while I was inside.

I found their way of selling chickens most interesting. An African appeared at the kitchen door with a dome-shaped cage on one carrier of his bicycle. Plunging in his hands, he produced several fluttering and squawking birds for my inspection. The price was usually about two shillings and sixpence. At first I was taken aback not being an expert at judging live chickens, but with the cook's assistance I chose one. They were a skinny lot and it was usual to tie them up to a shady tree, feed them up for a week or two to fatten them up. One day Sylvia came running into the house telling me the chicken had run away. The children had been throwing soil at the poor thing and in desperation it managed to get away. Hastily calling my staff, I sent them off in pursuit of our Sunday lunch. There was great excitement with other servants joining in the chase. The cook returned in triumph holding aloft the defeated chicken. I gave up after that and bought our lunch from the butcher.

We had a large garden but no-one had a fence or a gate. Delivery boys rode straight across, taking the easy way to next door. At first, I rushed out feeling very indignant; the carrots and beans getting a bashing; but it made no difference. The next day they did it again. I became philosophical about this and many other things too. It was a debatable point whether to keep chickens or not with this 'open plan'. We did try it for a while but the eggs seemed few and far between. When neighbours told us that snakes were attracted to them, we gave up. Africans came round selling 'eggis'. The usual way to test them was to place them in a bowl of cold water; the good ones sinking to the bottom and the stale floating to the top. I was never sure which way round it was but always produced the bowl of water to show what a good housewife I was, or so I thought. Green beans were brought to the door tied up with grass in bundles. Peas were measured out from a sack on his bicycle. Compared with South Africa I did not have many round-selling vegetables. The majority brought carved wooden curios, elephants, tick birds and crocodiles. It was quite common to look out of the window and see a boy standing outside holding something out for sale not saying a word until I noticed him.

I enjoyed the novelty of life in Lusaka but I missed the walks to the shops. We were a long way from town and I had to watch that we did not run out of essentials. Most people ran monthly accounts and the shops sent the boys round each morning with an order book. The goods arrived in the late afternoon, the frustrating part was finding 'regret' scrawled over many items. Curious mistakes occurred. One day I ordered plate powder of a well-known make to clean the silver — they sent me Steradent — wrong plate. The milk was pasteurised and brought round in bottles by native boys with pushcarts. We had a great deal of trouble over this as it was common knowledge that they would often pour some of the milk into another bottle and top up with water. As the water usually came from a ditch, it was enough to put anyone off milk for evermore. We solved our problem by collecting it from the dairy. Training African servants was no light matter; without supervision, they washed the dishes in cold water and the state of the tea towels was disgusting. I had to almost stand over them to get the towels boiled. Given time and patience however, they grew to be very useful. The disappointing part was they changed jobs frequently. When we asked why they wanted to leave, we usually got the reply that they wanted to 'make change'. When applying for work they had to produce a chitupa (a kind of identity work card) giving particulars of his tribe, village, etc., and the names and signatures of former employers. Some of them also produced a small notebook with references. It was common practice to loan a good one out to their friends. The chitupa gave the tribal name, but the reference probably referred to him as John or James, and it was no easy matter to sort this out. Difficulties arose through not knowing their language. So many different vernaculars were spoken. I bought an English/Bemba phrase book, and the next boy spoke Nyanja. Misunderstanding arose through this, sometimes quite funny. One day we were presented with a strange-looking tart. He had used carrots instead of currants. The wood was piled outside and in the rainy season brought in and placed overnight in the oven to dry. One day our fridge had gone wrong and I noticed that the butter appeared to have been melted and set again. When I asked the young houseboy what he had done with it, I was told he had put it in the oven to dry. He dried the wood, so why not the butter? I had no answer for that one.

The servants lived in a small house at the bottom of the garden. It was called a kia (incidentally our toilet was called the piccanin kia and always referred to as the P.K.). They had a small kitchen, lavatory and wash place. This was for one family; we had to apply for rooms in the African compound for the others. We supplied a uniform; usually trousers and a long white tunic called a kanza. The cook had a large chef's hat. The houseboy a round hat. The garden-boy khaki shorts and shirt, and no hat. They had ration money each Friday to buy their food, and were paid wages at the end of the month. We had responsibilities to them and when any of the family was ill we either bought medicine from the chemist, or took them to hospital if it was serious.

When we arrived in Lusaka, towards the end of the winter, everywhere was dry and yellow. During the daytime it was sunny and warm, but chilly in the evenings. October was springtime, and despite the fact that not a drop of rain had fallen for six months, things started to spring to life. The trees were most attractive, but in reverse to an English spring. As the new leaves appeared on the trees, they were russet and gradually changed to green. In the older residential part of town, the jacaranda trees were a lovely sight in springtime. First a mass of lavender-coloured blooms against a cloudless blue sky, followed by the green leaves. As the flowers fell to the ground, everywhere was a carpet of deepest blue. After that came the flamboyants with their vivid orange red flowers and the tecoma with deep yellow blossoms. Tiny wild orchids sprang up overnight. The grass was burnt from the previous autumn, leaving blackened ground, but after the first rains in November, everything was green again.

Most of our houses stood in large gardens set back from the road and at first I felt rather isolated. The one bus only catered for the workers and arrived in town at eight o'clock and left again at noon. Time hung heavily on my hands with so little to do. Once or twice I went on the bus but the town was small, the cafe full of flies and to hang about for several hours was tiring in the heat. In August the climate was lovely, but in October and early November, it grew very oppressive. Flashes of lightning appeared in the evenings, but no rain until mid-November. The first time we heard rain thudding onto the tin roof, we dashed outside. Who would have thought that I could be so overjoyed to see it raining. Eventually our goods arrived and we settled in; the snag being that I did not have enough to fill my days. Breakfast was over by eight o'clock, then a leisurely bath and potter round the garden. After that I supervised the houseboy, gave the cook his instructions for lunch. Sylvia made friends with children nearby and was quite happy playing in the garden, but I felt lost. Many of the women went to work in the government offices as there was a shortage of skilled office workers. I talked it over, a neighbour offered to have Sylvia to play with her two children and I applied for a job.

Although not quite eight o'clock in the morning, it was already very hot as I walked down the bush path through the knee-high grass to my new post. Reaching the primitive thatched building where I was to work, I was suddenly confronted by an elderly African standing smartly to attention. He saluted saying "Morni Mamma." I felt slightly embarrassed in my cotton dress, bare legs and sandals — surely this greeting was more in line with Government House. He wore a black tasselled fez, khaki bush shirt and shorts. Thin bony legs and gnarled toes completed the picture. His salute had been drilled into him during war service in the North African campaign. With a broad grin that accompanied the proceedings, I'm sure he enjoyed every minute of it. Talking of grins, he had only two teeth; one each side in the upper jaw. The office had bare cement floors with the odd rush mat and we worked on kitchen tables. His first job was to sweep out the offices and shake the matting. Preparations were then made for morning tea. There were lots of trees around. First he would collect the pieces of wood for the fire. Crouching in a corner of the veranda, he made the fire between a few bricks. The kettle went on next, as puffing and blowing he coaxed the flames. He was a willing messenger coming smartly to the office when called, but oh his tea, it was dreadful. Somehow or other, rainy season or dry season, it always tasted of disinfectant. Why this was I never found out as we had no disinfectant at the office. However, we survived. By mid-morning he got sleepy and would sit on his box under a nearby tree, chin on chest nodding off.

I was fortunate in my work as it fitted in with my business training and was allied to my love of books. The Government of Northern Rhodesia and with assistance from overseas funds had started a Publications Bureau. The aim was to encourage Africans to write books for their own people and to assist in the publication. One of the many things lacking was a supply of suitable books; apart from school textbooks, there was very little to offer them. There were four main vernaculars in the country, and many other lesser-known ones. The first step was to recruit a staff of reader-translators who could take simple stories already published in English and translate them. African folklore and popular stories had been handed down by word of mouth from generation to generation. It was possible to write these down, edit and prepare for publication. We had competitions from time to time. Piles of manuscripts arrived, laboriously written out in school exercise books or on scraps of paper. Coloured drawings would also arrive, illustrating the various characters in the story. After weeding out the most promising ones, the final batch was often dispatched to a missionary on an out-station who knew the language and understood the people there and what would be most likely to appeal to them.

One of our staff was a young man from England, who came out with his wife and small son. He pitched a tent in one of the outlying areas and lived among the local people, absorbing their customs and perfecting his knowledge of their language. He listened to their stories and when he came to our office, started to produce them in a style suitable for publication. All this cost a considerable amount of money and the financial side had to be carefully vetted. It was obvious that no publisher could take the risk of an unknown and poor market. There were two ways of arranging production. One was for a complete edition to be printed. Missionary presses already producing school books were able to undertake some of the work. The difficulty here was that a fairly large sum of money was tied up for an unknown period until the cash came in from the sale of the books.

The second method was the one most frequently used. The population figures for a particular area were carefully studied. The Bureau would guarantee to purchase a certain number of copies over a fixed period, varying from two to five years. The publisher would invest in a book knowing that they would be purchased over a fixed period.

The next problem was to arrange for the books to reach as many people as possible. The Copperbelt district was where we expected the quickest result, as the average mineworker was better off than his brother, who remained in the village tending the crops. Small rural bookshops were built of simple construction with a thatched roof, similar to the average African house. It was an interesting job organising and checking stocks. The idea of buying a book for pleasure, was a new idea and slow moving at the beginning. Two of our best sellers were *'Banja Lathu'* and *'Kalulu'*. The first told the stories of customs and traditions of the people. The second was the African name for the hare and was similar to the adventures of Brer Fox and Brer Rabbit. Another popular range was how to do things. These ranged from *'HOW TO GROW CROPS', 'HOW TO COOK'* and *'HOW TO SEW'*.

After a time we became more ambitious and decided to produce illustrated covers. We held a competition at an African teachers' training school about forty miles from Lusaka. This search for talent was extremely interesting and we were pleasantly surprised at the quality of the work. In some cases it was obvious that the artist was suitable for further art training, and this was arranged. Attractive pictures in oils and watercolours were sometimes offered for sale. I have a pleasant watercolour of a typical African scene, which still gives me a great deal of pleasure and reminds me of those days.

Our staff had increased by this time, and they were paid monthly. It was my job to work out the wages, cycle allowances, etc. With the form in front of me and the piles of cash, each name was called out in turn. The money would be counted out; any differences from the previous month explained and each man signed his name. When the name of Meluki our messenger was called out, he stepped up smartly to attention and saluted. The money was counted out into his hands. He removed the fez from his grizzled head, put the money inside and replaced the fez. Handing him the pen, I pointed with my finger to the correct place for signing. Very slowly and carefully he made his little pattern of squiggles. I realised that he could not read nor write. The rest of the staff were educated and standing behind waiting to receive their wages. He was a proud old man and to ask him to make his mark (whilst this was acceptable) would have hurt his feelings, so I waited as he made his pattern. Standing smartly to attention he always saluted and marched away.

As the Bureau expanded, the question of increasing sales was uppermost in our minds. Many people lived in the bush and communications were a problem. It was decided that we should purchase a van and fit it up as a travelling bookshop. All kinds of vehicles were studied to find one that would stand up to the corrugated dirt roads and narrow bush tracks. Eventually the van was ready, fitted up and raring to go. Members of our staff were trained as salesmen, simple methods of stock lists and sales sheets to be handed around. The salesman's job was a popular one. It usually meant that he would be able to return to his village where he had contacts and sell the books to his friends. The books were counted and arranged in the van; the driver given a cash float and money for expenses for himself and the salesman. One of our books was called *'Tiyeni Ku Mudzi'* which translated meant, *'Let's Go Back to the Village'*. It was a title that always sprang to my mind as the van was driven away with its large sign of MABUKU painted on the sides.

All kinds of problems cropped up as we expanded. An animal story about a lion was very popular. To have the same design on the cover was an economy when it was printed in different languages. Then there was the danger of the different books becoming mixed up. Out of this arose the idea of each vernacular having a different coloured cover. To the layman this may sound a simple solution but many discussions took place over this. Superstitions and old customs had to be taken into account; some colours were not acceptable to certain tribes. If the wrong colour was chosen no-one would buy the book. Storage became a headache as time went by. The guarantee periods expired and in some cases we had to buy the remainder of the stock. On the other hand, some were best sellers and ran into two or three editions.

Getting to the bank was a problem for all of us. Our salaries were paid direct into the bank each month and the banks were only open in the morning. We were in the habit of giving Meluki our cheques to obtain some cash to pay the servants, etc. In his black fez, he carefully placed the cheques and the note authorising him to receive the money. He stuffed the linen bag into his pocket and pedalled away the four miles or so to town. Our staff had increased and without thinking of the larger sum involved, we all gave him our cheques to cash. When it was time to go home for lunch, Meluki had not returned. No-one thought he had taken off with the money; we knew him too well, but worried in case something had happened to him. Returning to the office at two o'clock, there he sat under his usual tree, the linen bag between his bony knees. He had gone without his meal rather than risk anything happening to the cash. The same could not be said of his attitude towards tea and sugar. In his opinion they were meant to be 'shared'. In spite of the fact that tea and sugar were doled out each morning and afternoon, it had a surprising habit of shrinking. Why worry, what did a small amount of tea and sugar matter measured against such loyalty?

A few weeks after we arrived in Woodlands, we were invited to a meeting of the local residents' association. This had been formed for people to get together for entertainment and sport, as we were rather isolated from the town. The residents had already made a tennis court and a slide for the children. I had not realised that the evenings were so long; darkness fell between six and seven, according to the season. Something had to be done to pass the time away. We met in one another's houses for whist drives, dances, etc. I was asked to take on the job of entertainments organiser and promised to give it a try. Sitting by the tennis court one Saturday afternoon, a resident came up to me and said what a pity it was that we had no Sunday School for the children. I suppose this came in my province, so I contacted the padre of the Anglican Church. He came to see me and said he would be very pleased to arrange something, only where could they have it? Our large veranda was considered suitable and we had a regular little school of about a dozen children. Philip was made responsible for arranging the chairs and borrowing from the neighbours when required and giving out the hymn books. Sylvia, I considered too small to attend, but she stood on a chair in the lounge and watched from the window every Sunday morning. Residents were often transferred to other districts and our area was known in the end as the transit camp. Committee members were constantly changing, but the association survived.

November 5th is a day that I shall remember for a long time. We had planned to pool our fireworks and have a braaivleis with sausages, etc. Early in the morning, I went into Sylvia's bedroom to get her up and ready for nursery school. I expected her to follow me to the bathroom, but she called out cheerfully, "Mummy there is a snake in my bedroom." We often saw little shiny black things with lots of legs, about four or five inches long. The children called them Chungalulus, but she called them snakes. I went back, expecting to see one of these harmless creatures. To my horror, just inside the bedroom was a big green snake, curled in a ring, fast asleep. How I missed stepping on it is a mystery. My first thought was not to frighten her. Making the understatement of all times, I said "Yes, so it is, let's go and tell cook." Taking her firmly by the hand we walked past it, through the house to the kitchen. I said to our African cook "Come quickly James, bring a spade to kill a snake in piccanin donah's bedroom." My husband was away but I thought an African male would be quite used to such an emergency. Standing at a safe distance I waited, watching the bedroom door for the snake to appear. He seemed a long time coming. To my amazement he appeared with a packet of blancmange in his hand. Oh the problems of the English language! In my excitement I must have spoken too quickly. Seeing the snake, he dashed back for the garden spade and killed what turned out to be a green mamba. When I told my story at the office, someone asked if I had burnt it, as otherwise the mate was liable to come looking for it. Oh dear, my snake was in the dustbin.

During the afternoon, we had a thunderstorm, and as usual the electricity went off. The storm abated and we were able to have our fireworks and hot dogs, but I was not too keen on walking among the bushes in the dark. Arriving back into the house, the power was still off and walking through the rooms with a candle, was not the happiest night of my life.

I always baked a Christmas cake, even during the war years, and the ingredients were all to hand to make a real fruity one once more. My problem was how to adjust the wood-burning stove for a long slow bake. I arranged with the cook to stay in the kitchen one Sunday afternoon to regulate the stove. The cake went in the oven and from time to time I popped round the door to see if all was well. Yes, there he sat on the floor, back to the wall, legs and bare feet sprawled out, a steady warmth coming from the stove. The cake was a success and giving him a tip, he went off quite happily for the rest of the day. He was most upset when he came in the following morning. My ex-houseboy who had been sacked for drunkenness had been around making trouble. Walking into the servants' quarters he had drawn out a long knife and told the cook's wife that at two o'clock the next day he was going to kill her husband. He produced a pound note from his pocket and said that was the money to pay the fine. His idea of justice seemed rather strange but naturally we could not ignore this threat and informed the police. The poor cook was terrified but fortunately the would-be murderer did not return.

On Christmas morning we invited a few neighbours in for drinks. As they were arriving, an African band marched into the garden to entertain us. The front ranks were dressed in smart suits; the rest, in white shirts and shorts, and wore brilliantly-coloured football stockings. They played various instruments shaped like horns and rattled bones and then performed a tribal dance. It was an unusual start to our Christmas festivities and most entertaining. In spite of the heat, we had the usual Christmas dinner. We had a laugh over the pudding. Len poured the brandy over it, set it alight and rang for the houseboy. He asked him what he had done to the pudding. The look of amazement on his face when he saw the burning pudding was impossible to describe. We explained that it was our English custom. No doubt he thought that we were mad, making a nice fruit pudding and then burning it. When I heard the king's speech and the broadcast round the world, I felt very homesick for my people and the old familiar things. In the evening we went to a party and cheered up as practically everyone was from home and we all made the best of things and had a jolly time. Homesickness can hit very hard and nothing could be done about it but shrug it off.

Permanent houses were being built not far from us, and we applied for one. The big attraction to me was the indoor flush sanitation instead of our revolting bucket system. We made a record move as we were given the keys at lunch time and moved in early the following morning. The goods and chattels were always moved on an open lorry and consequently it was preferable to have fine weather. Our moving day was in April when the rains had normally finished, but not this time. We loaded up the fridge, carpets, rugs and radiogram in fine weather, and the first load moved away. Ominous black clouds suddenly appeared and the rain came down in torrents. We had lots more to move, including pillows and blankets, and spent the rest of the day ferrying them in the car. The outside of the new house was like a lake. We put a board down near the front door, but it just floated away. Most of the things were thrown into the lounge and the red cement floors were covered in mud. The bedding was damp and cook lit a fire in the kitchen, and we draped everything round to dry out. That was when we discovered that the kitchen stove was faulty; smoke was everywhere, so out went the fire. At dusk we discovered the lounge light switch was faulty. It was too late to send for an electrician, so I held a torch while Len transferred a switch from the passage. The plugs were all of the three-pin type and the old ones two-pin. It was quite a job making the alterations, but we visualised an early-morning cup of tea made with the electric kettle, and the radiogram pouring out pleasant music, as we worked to get tidy for the following day. How different it turned out to be. We returned to bed, thankful to relax. About midnight, Sylvia woke us, crying that her light was out. Assuming that the bulb had gone, I sat up in bed under my mosquito net and switched on the bed lamp — nothing happened. I reached for the matches in my handbag. In the rush of packing, I had crammed various oddments into it. There I sat in bed, turning out the contents in pitch darkness. The three brass monkeys from the pelmet were not much help, nor the serviette rings, but at last I found the matches. The next problem was to locate the candles. Groceries, pots and pans were stacked in boxes on the floor and it took the pair of us quite a time to find the candles. After giving Sylvia a light and making sure that it was safely away from anything, we went back to bed and slept soundly until the morning. I very much doubt if we would have done so had we known what was in store for us the following day.

We awoke to brilliant sunshine but no electricity and no working wood-burning cooking stove. We unearthed the faithful old primus and had breakfast. Gradually the news filtered through that the breakdown was a major one. Notices had been sent round to the offices and shops advising people to lay in a stock of candles or lamps as they would be repairing the boiler at the power station over the weekend. Africans had paraded the streets with notices in order that everyone could be warned, but we had been too busy struggling with the removal in the rain and had met no-one.

All the windows of the new house were a different size to the old one and I spent most of the day at the sewing machine altering the curtains. When darkness came, there was little we could do, as we had to conserve our small stock of candles. Reading and sewing was out and we went early to bed. There was no wireless; the cinema was closed and everywhere was completely dead when darkness fell. On Sunday the rumour went round that further trouble had occurred with the repairs, pumping would probably stop, we should lay in a supply of water. We were back to our days in South Africa with our water in the bath. On Monday our small supply of candles was finished and we cruised around the outlying districts looking for shops. This was the Easter holiday and the main shops were all closed until the Wednesday. Luckily we found a native store open. It was a tiny dark place, little better than a mud hut, but here was a shop that catered for people who never had electricity. Candles, paraffin lamps and charcoal irons were on sale. In addition to the candles. I bought a charcoal iron. I had never seen one before but cook welcomed it as an old friend. No newspaper was published and we wondered just how long the repairs would take.

In the middle of all this, I came up against servant problems again. I had trusted the cook to buy vegetables from a travelling van and had always given him sufficient money to pay for them. On the day of the removal, I had seen the van and told them of our new address. The owner mentioned that I owed him money and being in a hurry, I said I'd speak to the cook about it. He assured me that he had passed the money over and nothing was owing. I was sitting drinking my coffee by candlelight (not as glamourous as it may sound) when the houseboy came in and told us that the cook was in trouble. He had not paid the vegetable man; he had lost the money gambling and was going round to his friends to try and borrow the money before I found out. At lunch time, on returning from the office, I was told that the cook had paid the money. He had obviously got it from somewhere but could not be trusted and was paid off at once.

Another effect of the blackout was the large quantity of food that I had to throw away, as being the Easter holiday I had stocked up the fridge and all of it was useless. The lights came on the following evening after one or two false starts, and we felt like dancing in the streets. We had been under a total blackout from Thursday midnight until the following Wednesday evening.

During the next few weeks, I had three cooks. The first was pleasant and willing but obviously had never been a cook before, as boiling potatoes was beyond his capabilities. The second lasted two days. He started the family wash as we went off to work. Normally it was dry and out of the way by lunch time, but at tea time he was still surrounded by unwashed clothes. He said he was too old to do washing and asked to leave. The third, unfortunately for us, was light-fingered. I missed Sylvia's small knife and fork and on searching found them hidden at the back of a shelf; knives and forks were found at the bottom of the wood box, and a silver jam spoon hidden in a bag of salt. I had no choice but to discharge number three; altogether a most trying time all round.

Sylvia's birthday party was a pleasant affair, after all the years of austerity. How pleasant it was to see again, balloons, sweets, fancy cakes and chocolates once more, and to dress a little girl in a party dress and know that she would not be cold. After tea, the fathers arrived to collect the family at sundown and all stayed for drinks; altogether a children's party, was a happy family affair.

In Northern Rhodesia the 'King's Birthday' was a public holiday and the parade and ceremony made a great impression on me. It was a bright and sunny June morning as we set out with friends to the parade ground at the regiment. The acting governor in his immaculate white tropical uniform and white plumed hat, arrived with a mounted escort. The African troops marched along, their arms and legs moving in wonderful precision like a mechanical army. Then came the inspection of the troops and the slow marching along the ranks to the strains of the African band; the raising and lowering of the flag, the receiving of honours from the New Year and the announcement of the 'Birthday Honours'. Truly it was a corner of a foreign field forever England. Unless one has left the shores of Britain, it is impossible to imagine the feeling of pride and sentiment that is felt at such a time.

Burglaries were becoming rather common in the district. One morning Len dashed into the bedroom at six o'clock to tell me that we had been burgled during the night. I scrambled out of bed, heavy with sleep, and hurried into the lounge. The place looked a shambles. Cushions were thrown all over the floor, drawers in the writing desk were open and the contents strewn over the floor. Crumbs of flaky pastry and biscuits were everywhere. Apparently he had found food and walked around eating it as he searched the house. The gauze had been cut in the door of the ironing room and an entry forced, and although our dog slept there, we had not heard a sound. Returning to the bedroom, we noticed that the mosquito screen had been lifted up and my handbag was on the windowsill. Naturally the money had gone but keys, glasses and other items were still there. In a daze, we walked out onto the veranda and noticed a piece of blue paper that had been in my husband's pocket the previous evening. The thief had searched my husband's clothing but missed the wallet. Whilst we were talking, our neighbour walked over in his dressing gown and told us they had also been robbed during the night. The two men walked across to the neighbour on the other side and heard the same story. Had the whole street been burgled we wondered? But these three were the only ones for that night. In the next road a neighbour's shoes were missing. He had put them outside the bedroom door as usual for cleaning and by morning they were gone. He also took a good quality guitar and that was the thief's undoing, as a few nights later an alert African policeman heard it being played in the beer hall. He realised the quality and promptly arrested him. A smart piece of detective work on his part. The ironical thing was that we had decided to insure the contents of the house, had completed the form and it lay on the dressing table when the thief entered. One question on the form was "Have you ever been burgled?" We had written "NO" and had to alter it to "Yes" and send the form off with a cheque. Fortunately it was the only time we had intruders during our whole stay in Africa. A friend of ours woke up one night to hear the tinkling of money and opened his eyes to see his trousers disappearing through the window on a hooked stick. He gave chase in his bare feet but the thief got away.

A suggestion was put forward at our residents' meeting that we should start a branch of the Women's Institute. My husband was secretary at the time and wrote off to Ndola for details. The organiser said that she had never had an enquiry from a man before and thought at first that it was some kind of a practical joke. He promptly told me to get on with it. We invited the ladies from the nearby regiment to join us. When the speaker came down to help us form a branch, it was obvious that our house was too small and we were offered the use of a hall by the regiment. Later that year two of us attended the Annual Congress and Handicraft Exhibition at Broken Hill, and stayed for three days. We were met at the station and introduced to our hostess. A special welcome was given to us as 'The baby of the family'. Two interesting talks were given, in addition to the general business. I found Mr Roy Welensky (later Sir Roy Welensky) a most compelling speaker. We returned full of enthusiasm and one first prize for one of our members. The only snag was that as sub-chairman, I had to make a report, and I'm not that good at public speaking. On my return I wrote and rewrote my little piece, and heaved a sigh of relief when I sat down.

My next journey from Lusaka was a short business trip to the Copperbelt in connection with the rural bookshops that were being stocked in the district. Travelling was not easy as the trains were few and far between. The mail trains ran two or three times a week, and in between we had what was known as 'The Kaffir Mail'. This was the only one that fitted in with the times that I could make my trip. I arrived at the station at midnight; the place was almost deserted; no platform, and a few dim lights burning. After waiting for some time, I saw the light from the approaching train. All the trains had a powerful searchlight on the front of the engine to pick out any stray elephants or other game on the line. The train was packed to overflowing with singing Africans. What had I let myself in for I thought anxiously, as at first I could not see a European in sight? Peering into the carriages I eventually found one coach with a few white passengers and climbed aboard. I had a compartment to myself and settled down in my bunk for the night. There were numerous stops, the train pulling up with a sickening lurch almost throwing me to the floor. There was no dining car and I had taken a flask and sandwiches to tide me over breakfast. To my surprise, the conductor came round taking orders for breakfast. He told me that travellers could take breakfast at a hotel on the way. He phoned the orders through at a wayside halt. When we reached the station, some of the passengers alighted and strolled up the road to the hotel. Meanwhile we waited. It was a leisurely way of making a trip but hard lines on anyone in a hurry.

Our Bureau had a branch in Nyasaland and it had been suggested several times that I should go over there to sort out various stock problems. Eventually I agreed to go on condition that I took Sylvia with me and I would pay her expenses. At the last moment we discovered that yellow fever injections were necessary, and off we went to the hospital once more for injections. Each year Philip had a typhoid booster injection through the school, and then brave Mum took Sylvia to the hospital for hers. I have never been keen on the needle, but always went first and put on a brave front; which is more than could be said for Sylvia. She hated it and loud screams echoed round the building as the needle went in.

The Nyasaland trip was the first time that I had flown, but that was the only way to get there. First we flew to Salisbury; a lovely city compared with Lusaka. All the shops were decked out for Christmas. We wandered around for a time and stayed at an hotel overnight. The air trip to Blantyre was pleasant and smooth. It seemed strange to look out of the window and see the beautiful Mlanje Mountain alongside. Chileka Airport was quite a distance from Blantyre but Nyasaland being so mountainous, it was not easy to find convenient airstrips. The road wound up and down and around, and in many places was merely a track. We drove across rivers with planks placed over rotting boards and dashed down hills with blind corners at the bottom, but the taxi arrived without mishap. Nyasaland was a most beautiful country, with its lovely mountains in a lavender mist, and everywhere so fresh and green.

Blantyre was a tiny place; the few houses had neatly clipped hedges and pretty gardens, a few shops and a town hall and little else apart from the 'Information Centre'. This was almost a tiny museum and very interesting. In addition to maps and leaflets, were attractive curios carved in ivory. These were sold without profit to encourage local talent. The ivory earrings and necklace that I bought, remind me of that pleasant trip. I found an African market around the corner selling all kinds of vegetables. Hundreds of Africans were milling round and bargaining. I wandered around enthralled; no-one took the slightest notice of me although I did not see another white person. An old blind man was being guided along by a piccanin, the man resting his hand on the child's shoulder; neither of them were asking for alms. I travelled by road to Zomba, the capital. Large clumps of gum trees with their straight trunks, reached high into the blue sky; passed the tea plantations and coffee, with here and there, a small factory for grading and packing. We passed a number of Africans with large wicker baskets on their bicycles, carrying fish from the lakes to sell in the villages. Zomba was one of the most beautiful and peaceful places that I have ever seen. Its streams ran down from the plateau; the houses built terrace style on the hillsides, and all around the perfect setting, the misty mauve of the mountains. I sat and gazed into the distance with only the birds and the butterflies moving; such serenity was there.

Back in Lusaka life was busy. The children in our area were growing up and there was little for them to do in the long dark evenings. We got together and arranged a junior branch of our association. We had no hall and they met in different houses and organised their own entertainment; draughts, carpet bowls, etc. It was worth the disturbance once in a while to know that the children of twelve and over had something to occupy their spare time. There were no government grants and youth clubs for us in Lusaka, so we organised our own. We had numerous activities. The Church Council, Women's Institute, Residents' Association and the Business & Professional Women's Club, all took up my time.

In January and February that year, the rains were very heavy. We had no problem as the nearest river, the Kafue was thirty odd miles away. News came that the floods were bad and we took a trip down to the river to see for ourselves what was happening. The authorities were concerned as the railway and road bridges were our only links with the south in that direction. The road bridge had only been built about two years. Originally it spanned the Thames and had been shipped out and erected. It was difficult to imagine the river reaching to the height of the bridge. It towered above the waters. Chunks of land covered with tall grasses, some with young game still on them, were washed downstream. Now and again a large island came drifting down the river. The tall grasses were crushed under the bridge and with a terrific swirl the whole lot would be sucked underneath to appear a few yards further down broken into small pieces. I shuddered at the strength of it and was thankful that our home was far away from the ruthless surging torrent of water. We walked along the railway line towards the railway bridge; it was like a vast lake stretching for several miles. Walking back to the car, I suddenly stopped, foot in midair; there was another of those beastly snakes. I just missed treading on it.

One Saturday we went to an open day at the Jeanes Training Centre at Chalimbana, about thirty odd miles away. The road was very rough and bumpy with large stones in some places and in others were patches of sand which sent the car skidding across the road. Young Africans were trained at the school as teachers, and others had refresher courses. Farming was also taught and all kinds of handicrafts from the making of grass baskets and mats, to weaving and repairing shoes. The wives and families of the students lived there during the course. The women were taught domestic science and the children continued their lessons. The attractions of the open day included parades of students and boy scouts and physical training displays. The smaller children sat outside in a circle making tiny houses of clay and painting them. Nearby others were learning to cope with money and had a make-believe shop. They seemed to be enjoying this very much. In the evening an excellent performance was given of 'Cry the Beloved Country', so real and touching in its genuine setting. It was often said to me what good actors they made; with very little tuition, they seemed to really be the person in the play.

June came and we were due for our first overseas leave. It was a rootless existence for civil servants. Housing was in short supply and each house had to be vacated when leave was due and went into the housing pool. We never knew where we would go on our return. Everything had to be sorted out and packed in strong wooden boxes to be stored until our return. Every drawer emptied and every cupboard cleared — there was no room for sentiment. Old letters had to be burnt; toys and clothes were given away. Only the most important things in our life could be kept, and so farewell to a familiar house and garden. Souvenirs of that part of my life are few.

We had bought our first new car a few months earlier and decided to motor down to Cape Town and ship the car over. We set out early in the morning, our small Hillman Minx loaded to capacity. Once more we were packed and on our way, but this time we knew what was at the end, we were going back to England after five years. The dirty roads were rough on the first part of our journey with many detours around the hillsides. In Southern Rhodesia we drove along two narrow strips of tar, a slight improvement but still an uncomfortable ride. Notices appeared by the roadside 'Beware of Elephants'. We saw uprooted trees and large droppings on the road from time to time. Reaching our hotel on the first night, the proprietors asked if we had seen elephants on the way. They were quite sorry for us when they heard we had not sighted any. The last thing I wanted to see on that lonely road was an elephant. We usually planned to reach a town about six in the evening in time for a bath and dinner. The hotels varied from luxury to others that were grubby and thick with flies.

Sunday in South Africa was a day when no alcoholic drink could be bought. Stopping at a small place for sandwiches, we were refused lemonade to quench our thirst. Not on Sunday was their reply. The National Roads were all tarred, ideal for quick travelling but extremely monotonous. As we neared the Cape and drove through the Rex River valley, the scenery improved and it was very beautiful in the early-morning mist. At Worcester we experienced our first frost for years. It seemed strange to see folks wearing overcoats and gloves once again.

All was bustle in Cape Town, with its wide streets, high buildings and attractive shops. We had allowed several days there for making arrangements for the car to be shipped. Members of the book publishing firms with whom I had been in contact through the office, made us most welcome. We were driven around the beauty spots and invited out to dinner. They all expressed regret that it was winter time and we did not see the Cape at its best. The lovely rocky coastline was often shrouded in mist.

Our trip home was a big improvement on my outward journey which had definitely been austerity. This time, we had a cabin for three and there was a nursery on board and separate arrangements for the children's meals. We had not had a holiday for several years and spent the time lounging in deck chairs completely relaxed through a calm sea.

The ship arrived at Las Palmas at breakfast time; a lovely sight with its pink coloured houses dotted among the hills.

We ignored the waiting taxis honking away with their many-toned horns. It was more interesting to mingle with the crowd on the quayside. One persistent fellow walked alongside us with a tray of cheap jewellery slung round his neck. He kept telling us about his large and starving family and suddenly draped a necklace over my arm. I stopped and we decided that the easiest way to get rid of him was to buy it. Reaching the dock gates we waited for a bus to town. When the 'bus' arrived it was a shooting brake with a step at the back. The passengers smiled and moved up to make room for us. No-one spoke English and we passed over half a crown and said "Shops—town" and eventually arrived.

I was fascinated by the Spanish women in their black lace mantillas and the small girls with earrings and frilly dresses. We had been warned that the Church authorities were very strict about the type of clothing to be worn in the cathedral. No slacks, shorts or sleeveless dresses were allowed for the women, and men could not be admitted if they wore shorts. Suitably dressed, we wandered around the cathedral with its beautifully embroidered vestments in glass cases, and so back to the ship once more.

The following morning we woke up to a dull and windy day and the sea was quite rough. The nursery was not open and I warned Sylvia not to go on deck as it was far too windy for a small child. At breakfast our steward told us that they were turning the ship round as one of the crew was missing. The portholes were all closed, the ship gave a tremendous lurch and the sea washed over the portholes — we had turned. My first thought was to find Sylvia. As I hurried up the stairs it was like climbing a mountain as I clutched the rail. I dashed to the cabin — no Sylvia, had she been washed overboard? I was frantic, eventually I found her playing safely in a cabin with a little boy. Everywhere the stewards were unlocking doors and cupboards and relocking them. The loudspeakers were calling out for the missing man and issuing instructions and the ship was thoroughly searched. It was a rule that if anyone went missing the ship must turn back and search for two hours. Meanwhile all the ships in the sea were alerted. We stood at the rails gazing into that choppy sea wondering if he was down there. We never heard if he had fallen overboard by accident or deliberately taken his life.

England at last and after waiting for the car to be unloaded we were on our way to Leicester. How fresh and green everything seemed to us and how lovely to have long light summer evenings again. We rented a flat on the south coast for the greater part of our leave. The weather was disappointing, and the flat, though adequate and suitable for a summer holiday, was not comfortable for the colder weather. Unfortunately I went down with a very bad back and had to attend hospital for a month for treatment. Throughout my stay in Africa I had been troubled with nasty attacks of dysentery from time to time and had been advised to get treatment in England. In between I was quite well and tended to ignore it. During my leave it started again and did not respond to treatment. After seeing a specialist in London, I went into the Hospital for Tropical Diseases. The hospital took X-rays and were doubtful if I would be allowed to travel on New Year's Day as arranged. If I had to return to hospital they would send me a telegram. No telegram arrived and we all went aboard with streaming colds, looking forward to the warmth and sunshine of Africa. The weather was cold for the first few days, the sea choppy and the passengers looked a miserable lot huddled in travelling rugs.

I was looking forward to visiting Madeira, but it was not to be. We were later than expected and arrived in the dark, and decided to stay on board.

The ship anchored in the bay and the traders came out in all kinds of small craft. Many of them had burning torches and it was a wonderful sight as they sailed across the water. Reaching the ship, they swarmed up the ladder, were checked in and unwrapped boxes and bundles in a matter of minutes. Men were diving from the boats for money that was thrown into the water by the passengers. How they found it in the darkness amazed me. Beautiful Madeira cloths were laid out on the decks; fancy jewellery and boxes of cigars and all kinds of curios. Bargaining was going on all the time; prices dropped rapidly as the time drew near for them to go ashore. Everything was whipped away, the boats pulled alongside and the traders were checked off against the list. It was soon apparent that everyone had not left. Messages were broadcast in Portuguese and English asking certain people to report. This went on for over an hour. Once more the ship was thoroughly searched, the only difference being that this time we were still in port. Eventually the captain decided to sail. The following day my husband was an interested spectator when three stowaways were discovered in one of the lifeboats.

Every morning a small ship's newspaper was circulated to keep us in touch with the outside world. The latest news as we neared Cape Town told of heavy rains in South Africa and some roads being cut by swollen rivers. The sun was shining, as we collected the car for our long drive back. All went well for some time; we drove at a good speed; the roads were long and straight for the most part and had very little traffic. The roads were fenced but suddenly a young calf appeared on our right cropping the grass by the side of the road and to our horror darted in front of the car. Len swerved and braked but it was impossible to avoid it. The calf scampered away but the car was in a merry state. The bonnet had crumpled up like a concertina leaving the engine exposed. The roof rack had slipped forward and bent the sun visor onto the windscreen. Sylvia was crying and said that her neck hurt. I had visions of a broken neck, but after giving her a drink of water from the flask and comforting her, she was alright. Glancing around I saw that the car wheels were on the extreme edge of a twenty feet drop to a stream below. We had a very lucky escape from injury. A car sped by with folk from the ship; we waved frantically, but all we got was a friendly wave in return; they did not realise we were in trouble. We decided to drive the car slowly to the nearest town to report the accident. The Afrikaner police there were very curt and told us that we could be put on a charge for leaving the scene of the accident. As there was no-one about we had no alternative but to drive on and told them this. They said they had no vehicle; a police station without a car seemed rather far-fetched, but nevertheless they made my husband drive back with them in our damaged car to the scene of the accident. Meanwhile another officer produced forms and in an aggressive manner was asking my name, age, etc. Then came the question as to what had happened. I was sitting in the back of the car knitting when the accident happened. He asked me what I had seen, my answer was "Nothing". He was furious, screwed up the form and threw it across the room. If he had been more courteous I could have saved him the trouble. He took the precaution of asking Philip if he had seen anything and started again with his form filling. They were the most unpleasant police I ever had the misfortune to meet. No-one enquired if we were hurt or needed to rest. I often wished they would not blame us for the Boer War. I had it rammed down my throat on many occasions, as I pointed out once to a South African woman, "It happened before I was born, why blame me?" We were allowed to continue our journey; our main concern being the weather. If it rained the engine had no protection. We stopped at a small hotel for tea and drove on for about two hours when suddenly we came to a sharp dip in the road and in front of us a river in full flood. The posts at the side of the bridge were just visible above the water and the river was a swirling torrent. As we got out of the car, clouds of mosquitos proceeded to make a meal of us. The sun was low in the sky and we knew that in a few minutes it would be dark. I refused to cross the river; my husband was not very pleased about that. He pointed out that the last place was many miles back and if we delayed it might be several days before we could get across. Philip had said nothing but taking off his shoes and socks had paddled over to see how deep it was. It was almost dark by then and I could not see him. That settled it, Mum had to go over. It was a frightening experience to cross that long narrow bridge with water all around us and the danger of being swept away by the current. We made it; Philip was safe and sound on the bank and we spent the night at the nearby hotel.

On the last lap of our journey, we came to a river marked 'drift' and as it was dark, we decided that it would be foolish to risk fording the river and took the long way round over a series of rickety wooden bridges. We laughed over this incident as Len said jokingly that we were going round in circles and said we would put Philip out and see if we came back to him. Sylvia thought we were serious and was most upset that we should leave her big brother in the dark.

We reached our last hotel at eight-thirty in the evening, booked in and asked for dinner — sorry no dinner — Could we have sandwiches please? Sorry, no sandwiches. The staff had gone off for the night. What a reception after a tiring drive of four hundred miles. Dinner consisted of whisky and soda and biscuits, and lemonade and biscuits for the children. The biscuits were in the car otherwise we would have had nothing. The next morning after breakfast, the manager enquired if we had been comfortable. I told him in plain language what I thought of the lack of food but he merely shrugged his shoulders and said that the boys had gone off for the evening. I replied that I was English and quite capable of cutting a few sandwiches, if I had been allowed in the kitchen.

Arriving back in Lusaka, we stayed the night with friends as we had to wait until the morning to find out where we were to live. We were allocated a house, and started unpacking. As dusk fell, the room was filled with flying ants. There must have been hundreds of them flitting about. Apparently there was a hole in the mosquito netting and the light had attracted them. We put out the light and went to bed. We discovered that we had been given a temporary housing allocation and were to move out in about ten days' time. In the meantime we both returned to work and settled in for the time being.

Attractive houses were being built on the outskirts of Lusaka and several of our friends bought plots. We thought how pleasant it would be to have a home of our own again with no more packing up for leave. We drove around and almost decided to buy one. Opposition to Federation was growing; clouds appeared on the political horizon and we decided against it. We noticed that a number of things were missing. Several houseboys were dismissed as the cook always suggested it was done by them. The cook was clean, pleasant and well spoken. If I wanted to speak to him when he was off duty, he was usually sitting outside his house reading a Bemba version of the Bible to his friends. The time came for us to move out of our temporary house; we had been allowed to stay a few weeks longer than anticipated. It was just our luck that on moving day, the Africans had chosen it as a day of prayer. What the difference was between a day of prayer and a strike I never discovered. The staff did not go to pray and they did no work. It was their protest against Federation. No lorries or vans were available to move us. We moved most of the things in the car and trundled the radiogram and fridge on a wheelbarrow, leaving the firewood and oddments until things were back to normal. When we sorted ourselves out, my husband's shoes were missing and as we now only had the 'good' boy — exit the cook.

The next one was completely honest but had a weakness for beer and ladies. His 'wife' was a most attractive girl and I suggested that he teach her to do the housework. He thought it was a good idea as they would have two lots of wages. After a few days she decided she did not want to work in the house and was too tired. A few nights after this, we were awakened by screaming and shouting at the bottom of the garden. Sound carried in the stillness of the night and we had more sense than to go out to investigate. We called out for them to be quiet. I was amused to hear the story from a neighbour the following day. It was two women fighting over my attractive cook; both wanted him. I found out that the girl was not his wife; he had a wife and family in Southern Rhodesia. After that he sent her away, but drowned his sorrows in the beer hall. To watch him teetering across the kitchen trying to do the ironing when he was hopelessly drunk, was too much, and he had to go.

Politically things began to look bad; Mau Mau was still raging in Kenya (it started while we were on leave). The African staff at the office talked about it constantly and one said that he was prepared to die for his country. Talk of this nature was very unsettling, particularly when one had children. The problems were very great and I had a lot of sympathy for the educated Africans. The same restrictions applied to them all and the colour bar was strictly enforced. One of our staff spent two years in England in further education. He returned full of hope which gradually turned to bitterness. He once said to me that in England the word freedom meant freedom. I did not know how to reply except to agree with him. He went on to tell me that when he was in London he could walk the streets at midnight and no-one questioned him. Back in his own country he was obliged to carry a pass and not allowed out after dark without a letter from his employers granting him permission. On one occasion he needed methylated spirits for his primus stove but being an African he could not buy it without a letter from a European. He explained this when he asked me to write a note for him. This was rather a different problem, as originally this rule was brought in for their protection, as they were inclined to drink it with terrible results. Clerks in the office told me that men went around the compounds in the middle of the night waking folks up and bullying them into joining a political party. I had an instance of this when my cook came to me, very upset. A man had been round to his house and said he must join the party and pay two shillings and six pence a week for himself, the same for his wife and one shilling and three pence for each of his sons. This was a lot of money for him. They said if he did not join, he would be fined fifty pounds. Where they thought he could get fifty pounds from I could not imagine. I did report that incident to the police, but heard nothing more.

Federation of the two, Rhodesia and Nyasaland, came into being. There was a big political meeting in the compound not far from where we lived. The White Paper issued by the Government was publicly burnt; shouting, singing and the beating of drums went on throughout the night. It made me feel very uneasy. Instead of buying a home in Africa, our thoughts were turning to England. We saved hard that tour and planned to look around on our next leave.

Everything was not gloom however. The Rhodes Centenary Exhibition was held in Bulawayo. I was asked to go down for the opening to arrange a display of books for Africans and an attractive range of books on birds in Africa. (How I wish I had bought copies of them). I arrived two days before the opening. As usual in these circumstances everywhere was utter confusion. On the day, lawns and flowerbeds looked as though they had been there for years. It was a very large exhibition. I found it most interesting meeting the public and explaining the work of the Publications Bureau. I had a hectic time selling stamps. Why I got into this, I never quite understood? Staff was rather thin on the ground and I found myself selling stamps commemorating the Rhodes Centenary Exhibition and also Coronation Stamps. Collectors came from all over the world and we did a roaring trade from small packets containing a selection of the lower denominations, to whole sheets of various kinds. During lunch breaks, I was free to wander around the exhibition and enjoy myself. In the grounds of the exhibition, a large theatre was built and live shows came out from London. I well remember sitting waiting for a ballet performance to start and listening to the tuning up of the orchestra; I suddenly realised that it was the first time that I had heard live music in Africa.

To my delight, I was told that I could go down again to the exhibition in July when the Queen Mother and Princess Margaret were attending. Security was very strict on the actual day of their arrival; the public not being allowed inside the Rhodesia Pavilion where I worked. Out came the hats and gloves, so seldom worn, and in our high-heeled shoes we stood awaiting their arrival. Cameras flashed warning us that they were coming and we had a close view as they passed by. The Royal Party took tea in the Southern Rhodesia section of the building and arrangements were made for our positions to be presented. To my consternation we were moved around and I was to stand in front of the copper exhibit. Copper was the chief export of the country and was most important. I did not live in the Copperbelt area and had no facts at my fingertips. Meanwhile the lady who had taken my place on the book stand was also wondering what to say if any questions were asked. We were spaced out at intervals on the wooden steps of the large display stand. I made my curtsy without mishap and with a charming smile they passed on their way — no questions about copper.

The Business and Professional Women's Club flourished and we arranged a monthly lunch at the Ridgeway Hotel. It was obvious that we were going off somewhere, as we arrived at the government offices in our hats etc. in the morning. The usual greeting from the male members of the staff was "Here come the Professional Ladies."

The outstanding event towards the end of our second tour of duty was the visit of the Queen Mother. Crowds were everywhere pressing forward to get a better view. Europeans and Africans, standing side by side, seemed to forget the colour bar in their enthusiasm. The streets were decorated in an unusual way; African shields and imitation elephant tusks were made locally forming archways — no commonplace fairy lights for us. The school children lined the road from the airport. A group of Indians, the women in their beautiful saris, stood close to us. We took a shot on the camera thinking it would be an unusual picture to show back home. Today it is commonplace, there are thousands of them in my home town; how times change. Outside the government offices a number of African chiefs were waiting to be presented. They were impressive in their traditional dress, some of them quite old and very dignified.

The highlight for us was an invitation to the Royal Garden Party held in the grounds of Government House. It was a beautiful sight, everyone dressed in their best; the dark suits of the men contrasting with the gay summer dresses and hats of the ladies, and here and there a top hat was seen. African chiefs in their regalia and their wives in colourful flowing garments and headgear, mingled with the crowd. My one regret was that cameras were forbidden; what a lovely record we could have taken. The memorable occasion ended with the beating of the retreat and a presentation of silver drums to the regiment. This ceremony always impressed me in the splendour of a rich African sunset.

Around that time polio was taking its toll all over the world. We had a number of cases in Lusaka, some of them very serious. Sylvia went to playschool in the afternoons and on Saturday mornings as did most of her friends, as we only had morning school. Apparently some of the children had been in contact with the family of a polio victim. We called to collect her on the Saturday and the health officer was waiting to see all the parents. All the children had to be kept in strict isolation for the period of incubation. At first our friends knew nothing of this and immediately we saw a car pulling into the drive we dashed out to explain. I watched with anxious eyes as she played alone in the garden. Fortunately she was spared and later polio vaccine was flown in and all the children lined up at the hospital to take the drops on a lump of sugar.

Shortly after this, Sylvia became quite ill for nearly a week with a very high temperature. The doctors were worried as there were cases of typhoid about and one never knew in the tropics what it might be. It was certainly not malaria — we always took the tablets and throughout the whole of our stay in Africa none of us went down with malaria. At last, spots appeared and it was a bad attack of measles, leaving her much thinner and with a nasty cough. I decided to take her down to the Victoria Falls, a favourite holiday spot of ours. The Falls Hotel was a delightful place with large airy rooms and pleasant gardens. From the lounge we could gaze at the bridge over the falls. There was a party of Americans staying in the hotel at the time we were there. They had arrived to study African birds. I have never seen folks so well endowed with cameras. Most of them had three; one slung around the neck, another hanging from the wrist and carrying a third. In the bus on the way to Livingstone, one man said very loudly that he was tired of travelling the world and thought he would go salmon fishing the next time. What wealth there is in the world, but apparently it had brought him boredom. I loved to watch the baboons near the Victoria Falls playing around with their babies on their backs. They were however to be treated with caution as they could and did bite people. As this was a popular spot for tourists, there were plenty of curio sellers around with their wares laid out under the trees. Personally, I enjoyed wandering down by the river to watch the water rushing over the stones on its way to the massive falls. The roar and thunder as it cascaded down to the ravine below is one of nature's wonders. I cherished the hope that I might return some day to gaze once more upon its wonders, but alas Africa is a troubled country.

All the young men did six months' military training; part of it, the most rigorous, was in the mountains bordering on Portuguese East Africa. The discipline was a good thing for young men. My son was quite proud of his boots; boned until they shone. What a change it was for them after years of putting them outside the bedroom door for the houseboy to clean. Some children were adept at bossing the servants around. "Pump my bicycle up boy" was often heard. It never happened in our home.

Keeping a dog had its problems. There were several outbreaks of rabies, when a tie-up order was in force for weeks at a time. Our dog was tied to a long clothesline in the garden which gave him a fair run, but it was not a good thing for a dog. Nevertheless it had to be done, if they got loose, the police had authority to shoot them. Rabies is a terrible scourge; I trust it never reaches the shores of this country. There was a nasty scare when a dog not far from us was found to have died of rabies. The owner ran a small playschool and all the poor little mites had to undergo the unpleasant jabs in the stomach for rabies injections.

Leave time came round once more. Down came the curtains and pictures and the usual hectic clearing out and packing took place. Bed linen was a problem as this was needed until the last night and no-one wanted to pack dirty sheets for six months. We solved this by leaving them with a friend to be laundered and stored and did the same for them when their leave came due.

This time we were travelling to Beira on the east coast, involving several changes and hours of waiting for trains. On the way from Salisbury, the conductor on the train informed us that our luggage had been broken open. We arrived in Beira early on New Year's Day. It was chaotic at the customs and immigration posts. Most of them had been up all night celebrating. Conditions were the same at the hotel; the newest and best in Beira. A gala dinner and dance had gone on until five o'clock in the morning; porters were sweeping away mounds of streamers and very few of the staff were on duty. Eventually we were shown to our rooms and given breakfast in a small side room. We spent two days in Beira wandering around. It was very hot, rather dirty and smelly. Fortunately the hotel was very pleasant, large and airy; beautifully furnished; the crystal chandeliers being very attractive. I had a white felt hat with me which was becoming rather grubby and dumped it in the wastebasket. To my embarrassment, one of the staff came hurrying down the beautiful wrought-iron staircase as we were leaving, holding out my dingy squashed hat.

The ship was much smaller than the Union Castle liners; the crew and stewards were all Indian and the service and food was excellent. Our first port of call was Dar es Salaam, a lovely sight as we drew slowly into the harbour. The dazzling white sands and palm trees making a wonderful setting. The ship anchored offshore and lots of small boats were quickly alongside offering to take us ashore. It was extremely hot, but we enjoyed looking around. We found the coolest place to be the local museum with its tiled floors and shady cool rooms. Tanga was our next stop. Anchored further out than before, it was a twenty minutes' ride to the shore. There was little of interest; my chief recollection is the men sitting on pavements busy at their sewing machines. As we walked up the hill towards the town, the view of the harbour resembled a travel poster with the ship in the centre of the bay.

Next came Zanzibar, a place I had wanted to visit for a long time. We clambered down the ladder into one of the smelly diesel-engined boats that was waiting alongside. The small boat was packed with passengers, but I only saw two lifebelts. I wondered if they had safety regulations in those foreign parts? The usual hubbub greeted us on the shore, not least being the persistent entreaties of the local taxi drivers to take us round the island. We decided on an Indian driver with a Hillman car and set off on our trip. We passed the Sultan's Palace and stopped to take photographs of that elaborate white building with its ornate balconies and pillars. Some Arab women were walking nearby dressed in black from head to foot and heavily veiled. Our driver warned us not to take photographs, as it was against their custom, and would cause offence. Into the town centre we drove; the streets being the narrowest I had ever seen. In some places one could almost stretch out across the road and here we left the car and continued on foot. The tiny dark shops, with their jewellery and carved wooden trays and boxes, drew me like a magnet. Old-fashioned glass-fronted cupboards and glass-topped counters contained souvenirs of all kinds. Bracelets, brooches and earrings of Burmese silver were laid out in a tempting array. We bought a lovely carved wooden tray; the sections in the shape of water lilies; and rejoined the waiting taxi. We moved on to the outskirts of the town, past the residence of the British Governor with its massive wooden front door heavily carved in rich dark wood. The road was narrow but tarred as we drove past clove plantations, tall green trees with vivid orange blossom, with the sea making a wonderful background to the scene. Now and again we passed oxen of an unusual type with two large humps on the backs. There were many palaces on the way; some in ruin, others guarded by tiny cannons. Our trip planned to take us through the town, round the island and back to the harbour. The scenery was beautiful and we were enthralled by it all; the only snag was that we were feeling thirsty. We entered the outskirts of the town by a different route. The streets were narrow, and dirty water ran along the side of the road. The whole area smelt strongly of fish. At the far end of the street, a small crowd had collected. As we drew near, we saw a native coffee seller seated on the ground; a large brass coffee pot in his hands, and attached to the spout, a small brass measure. The Arabs waiting to be served looked in surprise as our car drew up with a flourish and the driver said to us "You want nice coffee --?" I have drunk coffee in various places but the thought of drinking the stuff in that filthy smelly place, was more than I could stomach. We smiled politely and said "No thank you" and he drove on to the harbour.

We stayed at Mombasa for several days. More passengers came aboard and the loading of the ship went on throughout the day and night. We would be awakened by a heavy thud as a load was dumped into the hold. Also the scaling of the ship took place whilst we were there, as labour was cheaper than other places. It was not altogether a peaceful interlude, but interesting to watch the loading of tea and coffee and copra with its peculiar smell. There were places of interest to visit and we were glad to move away from the docks. The trip to Nyali Beach was a beautiful experience. The silvery white sands and palm trees were a joy to gaze upon, but to walk barefoot was impossible, the sand was so hot. Further out at sea was a long coral reef with the blue sea breaking into bubbling white surf. We picked a piece of coral from the beach as a souvenir, much better than buying a chunk in a shop. We visited Fort Jesus, a jail in the old part of Mombasa. It was a sombre sight with its walls made out of the rocks and slits for guns. I enjoyed looking round the old port; here the pace was slower as we watched the loading of the Arab dhows; the men walking in single file with the heavy sacks on their backs. The sailing boats were soothing to watch and the buildings in the town with their domes and towers reminded me of my picture books of the Arabian Nights. We also visited the market with the moneychangers sitting at their tables. I preferred the ship's purser; it seemed safer, especially when we saw the notices 'Beware of pickpockets'. The noise at the docks was tiring and we were pleased to sail slowly away from the bustle. The sea was calm as we sailed up the Red Sea and it grew hotter and hotter each day. The only sensible thing to do was to keep as still as possible; the heat was very exhausting. It was dark when we reached Aden and seemed rather sinister with men sidling up in the darkness, tapping us on the shoulders and offering to be our guide. The streets were narrow and dirty and now and again I stumbled against a goat. The shops had all opened and were doing a brisk trade. Aden was a duty-free port; here was the place to shop for bargains. It seemed strange to enter a dismal untidy small shop and see all the expensive and well-known cosmetics and perfumes for sale at such cheap prices.

As we approached the Suez Canal, we anchored outside Port Suez. It was interesting to watch the boats drawing alongside stocked with a variety of souvenirs. A basket would be hauled up to the deck with goods for our inspection. If anyone decided to buy, the money was placed in the basket and hauled down to the sellers below. The novelty soon wore off and passengers drifted away. To my disappointment we entered the canal in darkness. It was bitterly cold after the heat of the Red Sea. Muffled in our warmest clothes, we stood and watched the lights twinkling on the banks nearby.

The following morning we were out on deck eager to see the sights. Towards Port Said the land was barren, but Port Said itself was very attractive in the morning sunshine with its domed roofs of green and gold, and the large ships anchored there. We were disappointed on going ashore as we were pestered everywhere we went. Boxes of grubby Turkish delight, sticky dates and dubious postcards were thrust towards us whenever we stopped to take a photograph. Worst of all were the small boys saying "You want my sister?" and holding out cards. There was a constant shout of "Genuine Scotch McGregor", whatever that was supposed to mean, I never discovered. Two drab little shops were labelled Marks & Spencers and Woolworths and did not bear the slightest resemblance to the chain stores of that name. We visited the well-known shop Simon Artz and made several purchases, one being a very attractive wall plate made of wood and beautifully inlaid. There was no bargaining there, no cracked and patched up curios; we could wander around as we wished without being pressed to buy. Making our way back to the ship, we came across the 'Gilli Gilli' men. In a matter of seconds coins were falling from our nostrils and flowers and chickens appeared from nowhere. I wondered if they had spirited the cash from my handbag, they were so adept at slight of hand. Returning to the ship along a swaying path of barrels with a rope handrail, we were exhausted. As we steamed slowly away, we took a picture of the statue of Gaspo de Lesseps, that had been erected in memory of the designer of the canal. Alas this is no more as it was destroyed during the Suez troubles a few months later.

The same evening, word went round that a young Indian passenger was missing. The ship was searched and it was presumed that he had gone overboard. It was a pitch-dark night and very cold when the captain announced this. The ship was turned round to search for two hours. The lifeboats were manned and put at the ready to be lowered if the missing man was sighted. The searchlights moved over the inky-black sea, but there was no trace of him. This was our second experience of such a tragedy and most distressing gazing into the dark waters.

The following day we ran into a bad storm. One moment we were down in the trough of the waves seeing nothing but sea, and then only the sky was visible. Folks were asking the bar steward what he recommended for seasickness. "Brandy on the Rocks" he assured the passengers. A short time later he disappeared and the smiling steward who had taken his place said "Oh he is always seasick." So much for his remedy. Sylvia was one of the few children still about, and I decided to teach her canasta to take her mind off the storm. We sat in the lounge, the wind howling in the rigging; now and again there was a noise like thunder as the sea washed over the promenade deck and crashed against the thick glass doors of the lounge. Many of the passengers were ill, including my husband. The stewards were busy assuring us that everything would be calm by midnight, as we were due to pass through the Straits of Messina. I woke to see the lights twinkling through the porthole and my husband standing in his pyjamas lifting his arm up from time to time. I wondered what was happening and discovered that he had a pile of sandwiches which he had ordered earlier on. He was building up his strength for the following day. A great deal of damage had been done; the captain decided to alter course and we kept close to the Italian coast until we reached Marseille.

No-one had told immigration and customs officials of our arrival and we stood on deck, the cases packed waiting to go ashore. Eventually they arrived with arms waving and loud shouts and we were allowed to disembark. It was January and a lovely sunny day as we drove off in a taxi with two other passengers. I had heard something of French drivers but what a ride it was, with no regard for speed limits, flashing through traffic lights at red, but we arrived safely at the hotel. It was a tall narrow building. The lift was open at the sides except for a grille which gave the feeling of travelling in a balloon as we rode slowly up to our room. In the evening we found an attractive cafe where we ate in a glorified greenhouse with soft lights and ferns; the place was warm and the food delicious. We arranged for a leisurely coach trip to Nice for the following day. Leaving the hotel at daybreak, we walked along the deserted cobbled streets to the coach station. Up and down we drove until we had a marvellous view of the island of Chateau D'If rising out of an incredibly blue sea. Along the roadside, the mimosa trees were in full bloom and we passed through numerous small fishing villages. We reached Le Lavendou at lunch time, and most of the passengers went into a restaurant for a hot lunch. We sat outside a cafe bar and had a pre-lunch drink, and went inside to pay the bill. The tables were set with red check cloths and each had a tiny vase of mimosa. I bent forward to smell the flowers. Suddenly a white-aproned barman called *"Attendez"* appeared and hurried inside. I wondered what crime I had committed as we waited for him to reappear. *"Pour vous Madame"* he said, his face wreathed in smiles and passed over a huge bunch of mimosa. I felt delighted and embarrassed, not being in the habit of receiving bouquets from strange men; but it was a kindly gesture much appreciated as I wandered off with my beautiful flowers.

We climbed the steep cobbled streets in search of food and bought butter, cheese and ham and large pieces of French bread for our picnic on the beach. The roads winding up and around the mountains afforded magnificent views of the coastline below. Meanwhile the driver gave a commentary in rapid French, describing the local beauty spots, which I could not follow. Fortunately my husband was well acquainted with the language, having spent part of his school days in France and he took the driver aside and asked him to recommend a suitable hotel in Nice. We had heard of the fabulously expensive hotels there and were getting slightly worried. He took us to a hotel where he stayed overnight on his coastal tours, and all was well.

Preparations were going ahead for the annual carnival when we arrived. Massive pictures in coloured lights were going up everywhere.

We took the train to Monte Carlo, a short journey of fifteen minutes. My first impression was the lovely view of the harbour with the houses tucked into the hillside. The place was almost deserted at that time of the year and was rather disappointing. We wandered around the outside of the casino, the view from the back of the building was particularly beautiful as we looked over the cliff to the beautiful coastline beyond. This we were told was where the unlucky gamblers took the plunge to their death. How foolish can people be with such beauty around. A small orchestra played outside, but the sky darkened, the piano was whisked away, and the orchestra disappeared as the rain came down.

We walked over to a cafe nearby. Inside was an elderly lady sitting alone and when she heard us speaking in English as we chose our cakes, she asked if she could help us. We moved to her table and were soon chatting away about Africa and our trip home. She told us that she was Swiss and when she heard we intended to go to Paris gave us the address of a fellow countrymen of hers who ran a hotel. She assured us that his terms were moderate and the hotel clean.

The following day we took the bus to Monte Carlo and found that the Royal Palace at Monaco was open to the public during the daytime. The guards, the cannons and the palace itself looked like something out of a storybook. As we walked round the various apartments I was once again lost in a torrent of fluent French spoken by the guide.

Soon it was time to be moving on and we booked seats on the train for Paris. The weather had turned very cold and overcast. We visited a delicatessen and bought "am" cheese, butter and French bread for the journey and also a bottle of wine and glasses. Reaching Toulon, a French naval officer entered our carriage and to my surprise he started chatting away to my husband. 'Where was the English reserve and silence in railway carriages?' I thought. I gathered that he had been to England at the time of the Coronation. He was highly amused at the number of snacks we ate. The English "So Phelgmatique" and constant eating. Now and again one of the men would be at a loss for the right word and out came pen and newspaper a little sketch drawn and *"Ah oui"* and off they went again. I was most amused but could not join in the conversation.

Paris was a great disappointment. The coldest weather for fifty years greeted us. The beautiful fountains had icicles a foot long; the Eiffel Tower was frozen and hidden in mist at the top. As for Paris fashions, all the girls seemed to be wearing cream duffle coats and hoods and thick black stockings. So much for my dreams of beautiful Paris I thought. But it was January, perhaps I had expected too much? We arranged to fly to London.

On the morning of our departure, tiny pellets of snow were falling as we took a taxi to the air terminal. Paris looked dismal and drab with its cobbled streets that day. All was confusion at the airport; the weather had deteriorated, flights were cancelled; but after a wait of a few hours we managed to get seats on a plane packed to capacity. As everyone was wearing bulky winter coats, that did not help very much. One bright spot was flying over the south coast of England; the sun came out and down below was the English countryside brilliantly white with snow. After the heat of Africa I thought this was marvellous, but it loses its glamour when down on the ground. The weather was bad for several weeks, but in the excitement of reunions I did not notice it too much.

Next came the time to find our bungalow that we had dreamed about. We had decided on Sussex, our favourite county, and made our headquarters at a hotel on Brighton front. From there we travelled around armed with lists from the house agents. House agents had a wonderful way of describing property and often we met with disappointment. At last we found a bungalow at the foot of the downs with views of open countryside and in the distance the sea. We chased the builders and solicitors almost daily until we were able to move into our new home. Schooling was a problem whilst on leave, as six months without studies is far too long, so Sylvia was enrolled as a day scholar at a nearby convent school.

Philip arrived in England after completing his military service at Heany. Looking fit and well he planned to travel on the Continent, staying at youth hostels en route. He had brought his lightweight motorcycle with him by train and ship, and planned an inexpensive trip.

Once more we were packing up; the old Jaguar was sold; it had taken us on many a good trip round the English countryside. We had planned yet another route back to Africa, and sailing from Tilbury our first stop was at Rotterdam. We arrived in a thunderstorm; not a promising start, and donning our raincoats we stepped ashore in pouring rain. Things improved however as we drove through the town, overtaking long lines of cyclists, and the sun came out. Passing through a Dutch seaside resort, I was intrigued by the wicker high-backed chairs on the beach. They seemed to have strayed from a Victorian conservatory; so different to our simple deck chairs. The Palace of Peace surrounded by its beautiful gardens was an impressive building; a beautiful name, but will there ever be peace in the World I wondered as we passed through the impressive conference halls.

Next on our itinerary was the quaint little town of Delft with its church tower in the square and the many interesting shops with their attractive pottery. I liked Holland with its friendly people and the cleanliness of the place. On our way once more to our next port of call, which was Lobito Bay, in Portuguese West Africa. The beautiful tropical flowers greeted us, once more the bougainvillea and hibiscus but the atmosphere continental and attractive. The shops closed for siesta, much more sensible than our way of life. We were fascinated by the workmen laying the mosaic pavements. The patience with which they chipped the small stones before placing them in position was interesting to watch and the results most attractive.

As we neared Cape Town, we had surprising news in the ship's paper. One of our deck hands had been arrested for a daring diamond robbery that had taken place in London just before we sailed. It was world news and he had travelled unnoticed for a week or so, but was caught and placed in custody. Crowds were waiting at the dockside to see him arrive but he was smuggled ashore and we never saw him. He was returned to England for trial.

The trains to Rhodesia averaged two a week and we were able to travel to the top of Table Mountain in the interval of waiting for our train. We had tried on several occasions to make the trip but it had always been too misty or too windy and the cable cars had not been running. The first part of the trip was made by bus, travelling higher and higher through the beautiful suburbs of Cape Town. As the road narrowed, we transferred to a minibus for the rest of the journey. Seeing the cable car coming down the mountain, I was petrified; it was so tiny hovering over the great space. I felt reassured when I saw photographs of the Royal Family making the trip in 1947; surely it must be safe I thought. We had been warned that it would be chilly at the top and we wore our warmest clothes, but they were wrong, it was extremely hot and hardly a breath of air; nevertheless it was a wonderful sight and well worth the trip.

The following day we were on the train once more, three and a half days of utter boredom, back to Lusaka still without a railway platform, refreshment room or toilet. A great deal of building and road work had been done while we were away, from a narrow strip of road we now had a treble carriageway. Multistoried buildings had sprung up on the waste ground. Lusaka had the air of a modern city with pavements and streetlights.

Superficially things were more attractive but the undercurrents of political unrest were disturbing. The population had increased; gone were the days when a walk down the main street, grubby though it was, meant the greeting of friends on the way. From a cosy village type of life, all was bustle. The African policeman on his box directing the traffic had been replaced by traffic lights. One unpleasant incident happened to us about this time. We had dropped Sylvia off at a children's party and were making our way into town, when suddenly a small African child of about two years of age streaked across the road in front of our car. My husband swerved but caught the child's arm. We pulled up in dismay. The mother and father had been walking at the side of the road not holding the boy's hand. There was a nasty scene as the man came threateningly towards us. No Europeans were in sight; everyone was in town shopping; but a crowd of Africans gathered from nowhere and surrounded us. We stopped a passing motorist and asked to get the police. It seemed an age before anyone arrived; the threats grew worse but no blows were struck. "I'll kill you, I'll break you" the man kept repeating. A doctor passing by examined the child and said that his arm was broken otherwise he was alright. When the police arrived he quickly dispersed the crowd and we took the three of them to the hospital. A friend passed on his way back from town and offered to come with us. The child did not cry but the parents were wailing the whole of the time; a most disturbing sound usually heard in African funeral processions. It was a genuine accident that could not have been avoided but it opened my eyes to the bitterness and hatred that was growing amongst the people.

Philip returned from overseas leave still with the motorcycle which had taken him to many places in Europe. He was given a transfer to an out-station which pleased him as he was keen to see more of the country. Knowing that the place was small, about twenty or so Europeans were stationed there, he chose a Rhodesian ridgeback for a companion, and complete with his kit, climbed aboard a lorry for his long journey to Kawambwa. Then we were three.

Married women in the Civil Service were classed as temporary. We were rather like the government houses; placed in a pool to be used where required. A return from leave needed some adjusting, usually a different house and often a different job. It was the custom for the men to report back and be given the following day off to move into the new house and unpack. On one occasion my husband walked into the office in the morning to report back and was told to return the same afternoon. An emergency had arisen and I had to cope with the unloading.

During my third tour, I had various temporary jobs, filling in for people on the permanent and pensionable staff who were on leave. One had to be adaptable as I found out one morning when I was called to take over an office without staff. The lady who ran the general day-to-day routine work and had everything at her fingertips, had flown to England that morning on leave. Her trained replacement had been rushed into hospital. Rows of filing cabinets — in-trays — out-trays — card index boxes, were all waiting for my attention. My biggest problem was the incoming mail, as I had to read it and pass it on to the person who could best deal with it.

I was ready for a break by the time our local leave was due and we decided to visit our son. We were curious about conditions in the bush and naturally wanted to see Philip again. As he was stationed not far from the Belgian Congo, we thought it would be a good idea to combine our visit with a trip to Elisabethville. Visas were needed and the leisurely way that this was dealt with was most frustrating, but eventually the necessary papers arrived and we set out on our journey.

The roads were rough, each passing car enveloped us in a rusty red fog. On and on we travelled, dust on the road and trees by the wayside, until we reached the border of the Congo. Our documents were read slowly and carefully, grudgingly stamped and we were waved through the barrier. The scenery was the same — nothing but bush, the only difference being that we had to drive on the right of the road.

Arriving at the banks of the Luapula river we watched as the diesel-operated ferry boat made its way slowly towards us. Cars were driven off, followed by a bus; next came the passengers with their blankets and assorted bundles. No-one was in a hurry; patience had to be cultivated in Africa. The ferry filled up with fresh passengers; we drove aboard and crossed the wide river.

From the river bank we were once more in Northern Rhodesia and drove on the left of the road. This complicated arrangement was necessary as a strip of the Congo known as the Pedicle jutted into Northern Rhodesia and had to be crossed to reach our northern province. We passed an African village now and again with its few thatched huts, skinny chickens scratching nearby and sometimes a goat or two. The piccanins played around and waved to us as we passed by. Sometimes we saw an old man wrapped in a blanket, sitting at the door on his mat, smoking a pipe. The rural Africans seemed friendly enough; they had not heard the slogan 'One man, one vote'. We had planned to stay overnight at Fort Rosebery with a young couple that we knew. Their small thatched house looked very attractive; the chintz covers, the bowls of flowers, the soft glow of the oil lamp, I could easily have been in an English cottage I thought. After a bath, a drink and dinner, we settled down for a chat. My idea of a peaceful country setting was quickly shattered when they told us of their unpleasant experience a week or so earlier.

Ann had gone into the garden after breakfast and looking round, she suddenly saw a leopard a few yards away. She dashed back to the house and managed to slam the door as the leopard reached the porch. The cream-washed walls showed the marks where it had clawed at the wall trying to get into the house. Their African servant managed to get away by the back door and ran to a neighbour for help, and the leopard was shot. I realised that life in the bush would not appeal to me.

The following morning we set out for Kawambwa. We had been given a rough map and eventually reached a fork in the road. The sign did not point in the direction we expected but we followed it for several miles. Reaching a small African village we stopped — called out 'Kawambwa?' and they all pointed the other way and back we went to the road sign. On close inspection we saw that it had been knocked down. Someone had replaced it. Why worry which way it pointed? Such was life in Africa. Nearing Kawambwa the only sign we saw said 'No bus to stop here' which was not a great deal of help to anyone.

Kawambwa was an attractive settlement with about half a dozen houses, (for Europeans), two general stores, a post office and garage. The boma was a long single-storied building with a thatched roof standing apart with its avenue of canna lilies and at the far end, the Union Jack fluttering in the breeze. Truly this was a British outpost where the flag was lowered at sunset and raised at dawn daily. Nearby was a prison and on the hour someone would come outside and strike a huge gong telling the time of day.

We saw no wildlife but no-one kept their dog outside at night since one had been taken by hyenas. The water supply was very primitive. A narrow stream bubbled along through a pleasant leafy glade and widened out in the centre of the village. Small fishes and various objects floated in the water. Each day a party of prisoners was marched down to this central point. The water was collected in tins and transferred to large petrol drums. Two men carried a drum each with a long pole between them. They were escorted to each house by a native guard in navy uniform and a bush hat; he always carried a gun. There were two water tanks for each house — one for the kitchen and the other for the bathroom and toilet. The lid was removed and the water should have been poured through a filter but they seldom bothered and if the guard was not watching poured into the tank. I was in the bathroom one day when a black face suddenly appeared at the window filling up the tank. The water was a murky brown as it ran into the bath but better than nothing and of course had to be boiled for drinking. We came to no harm, so probably a little dirt did not matter.

We spent a pleasant day at Lake Mweru, an inland sea that stretched into the Congo. We were taken by Land Rover as this was the worst road we had experienced and would have shaken our Hillman to bits. Loosely laid logs clattered as we drove across the primitive bridges. We saw several lorries laden with fish from the lake travelling to the Copperbelt. One lorry had broken down and the driver had to stay with it until help and spare parts arrived. At night he lit a fire to keep the animals away. The fish had definitely gone off, the stench was awful, and lingered for miles as we drove on our way.

The lake was a beautiful sight in the brilliant sunshine. Due to the abnormally heavy rains that season, some of the trees were partly submerged in the water, giving a picturesque effect. Two launches were anchored further out. One belonged to the Agriculture and Fisheries Department and the other for the District Commissioner. He would travel to the villages at the edge of the lake to carry out his inspections and see that all was in order. We were told that sometimes storms would spring up and things could be most unpleasant. Nearby was an African boat-building school. Some excellent boats were turned out there under expert guidance from a boat builder from England. These boats were used for fishing in the lake. The local beauty spot was the Ntumbatushi Falls. The first series of waterfalls cascaded into the stream at the roadside. We climbed up the path to reach another set of falls and on we went until we reached the top where the final set of falls tumbled into a pool before making its long descent to the stream below. It was a beautiful spot, so soothing to rest there and listen to the splash of the water. Someone spoilt it by telling us that one of the residents climbed to the top one day and came upon a leopard. I did not enjoy it after that and was pleased to get back to the safety of the car. It was a good spot for swimming, as being swift running, there was no bilharzia. Philip had been with some friends a few weeks earlier and came across a lioness with her cubs sitting in the middle of the road. No-one had a camera with them and they sat and watched until after a time she walked away with her family. We admired the leopard-skin rug that Philip had on the floor of the lounge and asked who had shot it. A slow smile spread over his face as he told us that it had been run over by a bus in the centre of the village; an unusual ending for a wild animal.

Driving back in the dark, we were expecting to see some game. I felt safe perched high up in the Land Rover as I saw two pairs of eyes coming towards us in the dark. It turned out to be an African walking his two dogs. The following day we set out for the river and the Congo. This time there was only one road or track and no danger of getting lost. We travelled for hours and did not sight a human being or an animal, only birds and butterflies, trees and dust. We reached the small hut of the immigration officer and completed the formalities. After that it was merely a rutted track to the river's edge. As we drew nearer, crowds of African men, women and children ran towards the car. Shouting and smiling they directed us to two strips of corrugated iron that led onto the ferry. The ferry was a primitive affair made of empty petrol drums and strips of wood. We drove slowly onto the ferry; Len got out of the car to take cine shots, his foot slipped on the drums and he almost landed in the river. After that we decided to take the rest of the film through the open window of the car. Long ropes were attached to the ferry and a line of Africans towed us along parallel with the river bank. They knew just when to detach the rope and climbing onto the planks at the side of the ferry paddled us across the river. About three-quarters of the way over, we came to some reeds; they drew out long poles and took soundings and paddled off again. The trip over took one hour. When we reached the bank we gave them cigarettes and three penny pieces (tickies) and the last we saw of them they were huddled together sorting out the tips. We travelled for miles and only saw two fish lorries. About halfway we reached a cafe and petrol pump and seeing the familiar Coca-Cola sign pulled up for a cool drink. Everything was the same except for the signs and language; no more English, everything was French.

We reached the outskirts of Elisabethville just before sunset. The suburbs were most attractive with large houses and beautiful gardens giving an air of luxury to the place. Our hotel was fairly small but modern; beyond the lounge was a well-laid-out garden lit by pale-green flood lighting, giving a delightful cool effect. We paid a visit to the lido and spent a pleasant afternoon by the pool. My memories of Elisabethville are the tables outside the cafes, the attractive but expensive shops, and above all, the bougainvillea growing around the houses.

We set out on our trip back to Lusaka and encountered the worst road of all. It was like driving on a riverbed with hard pieces of rock everywhere. The vibration and dust were most unpleasant and the heat intense. There was nothing to do but press on; not a garage or cafe in sight. Suddenly there was a bump and a bang, and off came the rear spring, with all the leaves snapped off. We got out, surveyed the pieces, threw the main part into the back of the car and bumped on our way once more. We eventually reached the border and although we had passed through immigration and customs only a week earlier, they could not trace the entry in their records. This was almost the last straw as they were reluctant to let us into our own country. The African in charge did not understand English too well; no European was available and it took a long time before they grudgingly allowed us to pass into Northern Rhodesia with strict instructions to report to our local police. We had the car repaired and after another two hundred miles were home again, dirty and tired but feeling it was well worth the experience.

We celebrated our silver wedding later that year and started planning our overseas leave the following March; the future looked bright. It turned out to be the most terrible time of our moves. Returning from a short visit to friends on the Copperbelt, we were delayed by a puncture and it was ten o'clock when we arrived home. A note was stuck on the door from the police telling us to contact them immediately. We picked up the phone — it was out of order. Dashing across to our neighbours they told us the police had called several times during the day. Something had happened to Philip — that was all they knew. The police would tell us nothing over the phone and promised to come round immediately. Shivering and trembling, I waited. Our first thought was the motorcycle. I'd always hated the beastly things.

To our horror we were told that there had been trouble with drunken Africans near to Kawambwa. A European policeman had gone out with Philip and another young man to calm things down. As Philip spoke Nyanja, they thought he could be of assistance. All three were viciously attacked. The other two reached the Land Rover and drove off for help. Philip had been beaten up and left unconscious. We were told that he had been taken to a mission hospital, was still unconscious and very badly injured. Communication was by radio and news had not reached Lusaka until the following day. A light plane was standing by to fly a specialist if needed and there was room for one of us to travel up with him. It was the longest night of my life. He must not die at twenty-three with his life before him. What could we do but pray.

Early the following morning, my husband was waiting for the Commissioner of Police to arrive at his office and was told that Philip was still alive; his condition had not changed. He was being flown to Lusaka Hospital. How could the sun still shine so brilliantly as we waited at the airport when all was darkness in my mind? At last a tiny speck appeared and the plane landed. We stepped forward as they lifted him out; the waiting nurse motioned me back. She probably thought the sight of him would be too much of a shock. Battered and disfigured, he lay unconscious as they quickly transferred him to a waiting ambulance. X-rays were taken, examinations made, and we waited to speak to the doctor. He promised nothing — we would have to wait and see what happened — he was very badly injured was all they could say. We were allowed to see him at any time and could stay as long as we wished. We talked to him as he lay unconscious and hoped that it would help — I think in the end that it did. For a time he would be quiet then the threshing about and shouting started again as he lived through the distressing event once more. The nurse gave him an injection and we crept away, ringing the hospital last thing at night and immediately we awoke from our short troubled sleep. For twelve days this agonising waiting lasted and then — we walked into the hospital and he smiled at us. That was the beginning of a long slow recovery. Once we were allowed to take him out to the cinema for the evening and return to the hospital. The day came to fetch him home but when we arrived he had had a sudden relapse; it was a bitter blow and set him back quite a time. After he was discharged from hospital, we began to realise that he was far from well. Lumbar punctures and tests were taken and he flew to Johannesburg for further treatment before he was really on the road to recovery. At such times one can only hope and pray, and I remember the days when we were able to go together to our little church and give thanks for his recovery.

    Meanwhile the political situation had deteriorated and there was a great deal of unrest among the African population. For the first time we heard of home-made petrol bombs being used in the town. Several shops had their windows smashed, bottles of petrol thrown in followed by lighted matches. Election time came, with two electoral rolls; one for Europeans and one for African voters. Threats were made against any Africans who voted. Armed police patrolled the corridors of the government offices on election day and lorry loads of police were stationed outside the building, but no incidents took place. Trains were derailed now and again, and stone throwing was common. The railway authorities decided to man a small observation car with armed police. This travelled ahead of the train looking out for obstacles and gangs of troublemakers. We also heard of several little girls being pulled from their cycles on their way home from school. We decided that this was not the place for our daughter and the thought of our leave was shadowed by the plans to leave her in England at boarding school. I heaved a sigh of relief as our train pulled out of Lusaka Station on our way to the coast. We boarded the ship at Beira and found the continental atmosphere of the Italian ship a pleasant change. It was a delightful break after the dark times we had passed through. Our stay in Aden was much longer than previously and fortunately it was daylight. The main shopping centre was a mile or so from the port, situated in an extinct volcano crater. We teamed up with a couple from the ship, and after bargaining as usual over the price, took a taxi to the town centre. The driver locked his car and acted as our guide around the shops; no doubt collecting a commission later. It was extremely hot and the town itself was very dirty. I watched a small child drop a piece of bubble gum; it fell into a filthy puddle but she picked it up and put it back into her mouth. The shops were very tempting, as being a duty-free port, prices were much lower than elsewhere. Shopkeepers stood in the doorways trying to attract custom. We walked round one of them;

stoles and scarves were hanging in profusion and jewellery and watches lay in glass-topped counters. Our friend from the ship noticed some unusual earrings with tinkling silver bells and picked them up to show his wife. Immediately the shopkeeper, a bearded old gentleman with an embroidered fez, was at his side, pressing him to buy at a high price. Our friend decided that she did not want them and knowing my interest in earrings my husband offered to buy them. They were far too expensive in my opinion and suggested a price. The shopkeeper held up his hands in horror and after looking at other goods we moved off, down the steps into the street, towards the waiting taxi. Suddenly we heard a shout and saw one of his sons running after us holding out the earrings. We could have them at our price.

After this amusing episode, we set out on a trip to the surrounding district. We were told that the water supply came from an oasis situated in a pleasant tropical garden. It had not rained for two years. Next we drove to the camel market; a most fascinating sight, but oh the smell; I was glad to move away. On our return journey we passed the shining white salt flats on either side of the road. We also saw various carts drawn by camels. What appeared to be a bundle of rags on the floor of the cart, was the driver fast asleep, the camel slowly making his way without guidance.

The ship by this time seemed like home; we were always pleased to return to our familiar surroundings; particularly so on this occasion as we had eaten nothing nor taken anything to drink the whole time that we were ashore. The place was so filthy we dare not risk being taken ill with food poisoning or an attack of dysentery.

We anchored outside Port Suez and some of the passengers took the trip overland to visit the pyramids and rejoined the ship at Port Said. All the Jewish passengers remained on board, tucked away in Central Africa the implications of the Suez trouble had almost evaded me. Once again the boats arrived with their souvenirs and we decided to buy a camel stool. It was hauled up in the basket for our inspection; the price agreed, the money placed in the basket and my husband called out "Alright?" The man below nodded and we released the basket. To our amazement the man below was not holding the rope and the whole lot just flopped into the sea. We considered discreetly fading away as they stood gazing at the floating basket and appeared to be doing nothing. However after shouting to one another, a boathook was produced, and the basket recovered and everyone was smiling again. A rather haphazard way of doing business we thought.

We did not go ashore at Port Said; I did not feel particularly safe in daylight and certainly it did not appeal to us when we heard that we docked at midnight. We crossed the Mediterranean in calm weather and blue sea; a pleasant contrast to our previous trip with tragedy and storm. We drew alongside Brindisi on a Sunday morning. As we went ashore about eight o'clock, the ship appeared to be parked at the bottom of the street; no lengthy docks to traverse. The cafes and shops were closed but the market was a hive of activity with mounds of fruit and vegetables. Close by was a display of paintings laid out on the pavement. A gay and colourful interlude which passed very quickly as the ship's siren blared out warning us to return. We stood on deck, watching the ship pull away from the shore, when we heard that a party of young girls had been left behind. They had hired a rowing boat to take them back to the ship as it moved away; a rope ladder was flung out and they had to climb up as best they could. The captain refused to stop the engines for them. Luckily they were young and nimble and managed to get aboard.

The following morning we arrived at Venice. To our disappointment it was raining. The beautiful buildings that we passed and the quaint bridges over the canals would have made excellent subjects for the camera if the light had been better. As we went ashore it was raining faster than before. The customs shed was a babel of confusion — no-one seemed to speak English, but like everywhere else we had been, we were eventually sorted out and moved on. We had been given the address of a hotel by one of our fellow passengers and produced the slip of paper to the porter. We were promptly whisked away to the nearby landing stage; a gondolier summoned, our luggage stowed aboard and off we went. I had never visualised a trip in a gondola in pouring rain and icy cold weather, but it happened. We sat huddled together under the canvas awning, our feet cold and wet and also discovered that it was a very expensive way of travelling. We followed the porter down a long narrow passage, but the hotel was a pleasant surprise. The manageress spoke fluent English and made us most welcome turning on the heat in the bedrooms. She was one of the most beautiful women I have ever met. Each evening she would open up the tiny bar and sit and chat to us. The weather improved but there was a chill wind blowing during most of our stay. St Mark's Square was the first place we visited. The shops with their lovely Venetian glass and fine lace were fascinating, but mostly beyond our pocket. We took the lift to the top of St Mark's Tower and saw Venice laid out for our approval; truly a beautiful sight to be remembered. We wandered around the churches, fed the pigeons in the square and watched the traffic on the Grand Canal. Speedboats, water buses and gondolas all passed as we stood there. The following day a guide called at the hotel to take us to the Island of Murano to visit the glass works. We boarded a water bus to the island. As we speeded across the water, we passed a Venetian funeral; the long dark hearse mounted on a gondola slowly moving out to the cemetery, a small walled island off the coast. At the glass factory they were making Venetian birds. It was fascinating to watch the different colours being introduced into the main piece of glass. It was held in large tongs as it was twisted and turned into the lovely finished article. The craft was handed down from father to son. The buildings were very primitive and reminded me of the village blacksmith of days gone by. We were taken to the brilliantly-lit showrooms, a glittering display of chandeliers, dinner services, dishes and glasses of all kinds. We moved on without buying and looked elsewhere for our souvenir of Venice. In a small shop in the backstreets, we saw an attractive ashtray with silver set into the pestle. We asked the assistant to pack it well as we had a long journey ahead of us. Laughingly he said he had made a football and tossed it across the shop to his assistant. I gave a gasp, those crazy Italians, but it did survive the journey.

Our next stop was Berne, and as we were anxious to see as much of the country as possible, we altered our booking to travel during daylight. The well-heated Pullman coach gave us an excellent view as we sped through the countryside. We flashed alongside one of the Italian lakes; a vast expanse of deep blue water glimpsed through the trees, and it was gone. Gradually the scenery changed from men and women working in the fields, to snow-topped mountains and tall pine trees. Towards the end of our journey, a party of businessmen boarded the train and sat nearby. They were a jolly crowd, laughing and chatting over their drinks. We had difficulty in getting the steward to change a traveller's cheque and one of our fellow travellers turned out to be a travel agent. He insisted on cashing the cheque for us and bought us a bottle of wine, typical of the country they told us, and to calls of *"Prosit"* they raised their glasses and wished us a pleasant journey.

Armed with yet another address of a hotel, we drove off. The difficulty was that it was mainly German speaking in that area and we knew no German. The first evening the dinner menu was a complete mystery to us; however a waiter translated the lot for us and took our order.

The receptionist at the hotel spoke good English and told us of all the best places to visit in the short time we had there. We wandered around the old part of the town with its gabled buildings and at the end of the main street the bear garden. We were told that we must visit the bear garden as this animal is their emblem. They were fascinating to watch, particularly the baby ones. Large signs were posted up in several languages asking people not to feed them sweet things, preferably apple or carrot.

The following day we took a trip to Gurtenkulm. Boarding one of the trams in the main street, we passed through the town, up the hill to the funicular railway station. The platform was built in steps on a slope and the railway carriages were like boxes one above the other. We climbed in and soon the train was making its steep ascent to the mountain top. On either side of the railway line were woods; the trees in full leaf, and others already in blossom. We glimpsed deer cropping the grass quite undisturbed by the train. Stepping out, one had the feeling of being on top of the world. In one direction was lush green grass covered in fat white daisies, and in the distance the mountains topped with snow, like the icing on a Christmas cake. Down below was Berne resembling a toy village with its churches, shops and houses, and the river threading its way through the centre. On the other side were the woods, with violets growing in profusion. The air was still, the sun was shining and various trees were a mass of white blossom. It was one of the most beautiful spots I have ever seen and peaceful beyond words.

Paris was to be our next stop and we arrived early in the evening. April in Paris is a lovely time. We strolled along the Champs Elysées and sat outside a cafe, watching the world go by. This was Paris as I had imagined it to be; gone were the duffle coats and black stockings of our previous visit; here were the trim Parisians out for an evening stroll.

The following day we called at the garage to arrange about the collection of our new car. They were most surprised when we told them we did not wish to take delivery for a day or two. The pace of the traffic in Paris was alarming and the thought of risking a brand-new car to go sightseeing, did not appeal to us. We preferred to go by metro or taxi. This time we were able to go up the Eiffel Tower and look down on the Seine with its bracelets of bridges below. We also spent a pleasant Sunday afternoon in the Bois de Boulogne, strolling along by the river, edged with chestnut trees in full bloom. All Paris seemed to be there that day; the river was a busy scene packed with boats. The last day of our stay in Paris was all excitement as the maid hurried to our room to tell us the new car was outside. The proprietor and his wife came out to admire it (we had bought a French car). The luggage was stowed away, the driver shook my husband by the hand and wished us bon voyage. Len's face was a study, after all his careful planning for a courier to drive us to the outskirts of Paris, they had not been told of this. After an involved conversation in French and sorting through the documents, he got in and drove us through the town at a hair-raising pace.

After that we were on our own driving towards the Belgian border. We stopped at Rheims and wandered around the lovely cathedral and then on to Givet where we spent the night. My husband was anxious to revisit the village of Fromelenne where he had spent part of his school days. I had heard so much of the place and the approach was amid pleasant green countryside. The village itself was a drab little place with ugly stone houses. The town crier was just finishing his round on his cycle and the womenfolk were standing at their doors listening at what he had to say. We went along to a small cafe bar and were greeted by a pleasant fresh-complexioned young woman. I asked if she spoke English and wondered why she burst out laughing, until she managed to say that she came from Yorkshire. She was married to a Frenchman who owned the bar. Moving on, we drove into the Ardennes by the side of the River Meuse with its long flat barges, and on through Dinant until we reached Brussels. There seemed to be two distinct parts of Brussels; the new part, rebuilt since the war with its modern railway station and wide roads, and the older steep narrow streets with their rounded stones — so difficult to walk upon in high-heeled shoes.

We planned to have a picnic supper on our way and stocked up with rolls, butter, ham, etc., and a bottle of wine. We made good progress on the autobahn until we decided it was time for our picnic. Things do not always turn out as planned. Pulling up at an attractive spot, I was soon busy buttering the rolls and preparing the filling; meanwhile my husband intended to uncork the wine. We had bought a penknife combined with a corkscrew as a souvenir of Venice and this was the time to use it. To our surprise, as fast as he turned the corkscrew, it straightened out until we were left with a more or less straight piece of wire and the cork still firmly in the bottle. We were determined to sample the wine at this stage and after picking away with a penknife, the cork fell into the wine. Nothing daunted, we opened a suitcase, found a clean handkerchief and strained the wine through it. I have never recommended Italian corkscrews since then.

Darkness had fallen by the time we reached Bruges; the market square was a blaze of light as a fair was in progress. A fair has an atmosphere the same the world over, even if the language is different. We were tired after our journey and all I wanted was a meal and bed; preferably away from the noise. We drove around the town losing our way several times and eventually found accommodation over a cafe. Sylvia naturally wanted to go to the fair; I wanted to go to bed; so off she went with her daddy, and I was soon fast asleep. The following morning was cold and dull, and after a quick look round we decided to press on to Ostend. We had been travelling for so long, unpacking and packing again in strange hotels, we thought of home and a settled place once more. We had planned to visit the tulip fields in Holland but changed our plans and made for England. What a contrast that was to the present-day rush of overseas visitors. The docks were almost deserted and a ship was due out in half an hour; we drove aboard without any fuss and welcomed the white cliffs of Dover as an old friend.

It was the best summer for years, and looking back on that holiday, it seems that the sun was always shining and the windows wide open. We had a delightful holiday; everything seemed so safe and peaceful in England. A general election was in the offing, but what a difference to the strained atmosphere of the Lusaka election immediately before we left. No armed police were needed to protect the voters. The thought of leaving Sylvia was pushed to the back of our minds as much as possible, but all was arranged, and the day came when everything was packed once more; the car delivered to the docks and we took a taxi to the convent to leave her in the safe keeping of the sisters. Saying goodbye to the family, seemed harder each time. My father was growing older. Would I ever see him again? Leaving both my children behind, was more difficult than ever. Parting to me was not sweet sorrow and never has been. I gazed at the wash from the ship as the distance between us grew longer and longer, but we had to go, a living had to be earned, contracts could not be broken. The end of the trip was rough; as we sat at dinner for the captain's special evening, the glasses and plates slid down the table; the rails were up on the tables and I watched as they slowly slid back again. It was very cold in Cape Town and blowing a gale. As we travelled along the coast, the sea was green and flecked with white horses. We were not warm for several days and consequently when we reached the Rhodesian border in mid-October, the heat hit us like a bomb.

For the rest of the journey the temperature in the car was never below a hundred and four degrees, and when we stopped at a cafe and locked the car up for a few minutes, the temperature quickly reached a hundred and sixteen. Driving along a deserted road, we heard a very loud bang. It could not be a blow-out we thought as the car was riding steadily. We had been away for months. Had the fighting started? We stopped, looked around, not a soul in sight;

the anticlimax came when we went back to the car. A most horrible smell permeated the interior. It was not gunfire but the flask on the back window ledge. I had forgotten to rinse the milk out and it had fermented and burst through the cup. We arrived safely in Lusaka covered as usual in perspiration and red dust.

Politically things seemed better than when we had left, but trade had suffered a setback. Jobs were hard to come by, particularly for married women, as Africans were being trained to take over. In the past, it had always been a question of how soon could I unpack as I was needed at the office. This time, there was no vacancy in Government service for me. Many Africans and skilled Europeans were also looking for work; a thing unknown in the past. The days seemed endless with so little to do; Sylvia was away at boarding school and Philip still on leave in England. The houses were well set back from the road and few people were about during the day.

Eventually I found work and was happier with more to do. The cinemas opened about eight-thirty in the evening and it had to be a very good programme to attract us during the week, as it was almost midnight when we arrived home. The local theatre club put on a play about once a month, and a drive-in cinema opened a few miles outside the town. We found this quite pleasant as we could sit in the car with the windows down and enjoy the programme. The weekends I found very boring; no shops were open and we were not particularly interested in sport. At one time we had wandered around the shops between tea and dinner on a Sunday evening, but gangs of noisy Africans put a stop to that. From time to time demonstrations took place against Federations, with Africans patrolling the streets with banners. It was wise to stay at home, particularly on Federation Day, which had been made a public holiday.

On one particular Sunday, Mr Ian McLeod was due to visit Lusaka and crowds of Africans gathered at the airport long before he was due to arrive. We heard a commotion in the road near our house and looking out of the window we saw streams of African men, youths and women with babies tied on the backs, shouting *"Kwacha"* (Freedom). We warned our servant to tell his wife to stay at home with the children as we thought that things might get out of hand. Sure enough, just after midday we heard the shouting, it sounded like the roar of a football crowd and was coming from the airport which was quite a distance away from our house. Apparently when Mr McLeod arrived, the crowd started throwing stones and ran along the road en masse after the car towards Government House. A man we knew was in his garden at the time and had to beat a hasty retreat indoors to avoid the stones and brick-ends that were flying through the air. On several occasions when we were driving along, Africans raised their fists at us and shouted *"Kwacha"*. The biggest danger was if there was an accident involving an African, particularly at night. Many of them rode cycles without lights and if he got knocked down a crowd would quickly gather and throw stones. The police force was strengthened but they could not be everywhere and nasty incidents took place. One Saturday afternoon an Indian shopkeeper had an accident with an African cyclist; his new station wagon was overturned and burnt out. Fires were started in the beer halls and the compounds; not on a large scale but quite frequently. Several Africans were waylaid, petrol thrown over them and set alight. Home-made petrol bombs were thrown through the windows of African houses, often because the victims did not actively support a political party and were moderate in their views. Churches and schools were burnt down, particularly in the Luapula province where Philip had been stationed. All this made us wonder how it was going to end. Various large building firms withdrew from the territory and a number of businesses went into liquidation or bankruptcy. The happy atmosphere we had known in the past seemed to have gone forever. Philip wrote to us saying that he had decided to remain in England and would not be returning.

Sunshine is not everything and the price of freedom from housework was too high for the danger and uncertainty involved. We decided to return to England and my husband gave six months' notice. Shortly after we had made our decision, the papers were full of the forthcoming independence of the Congo and hinted at trouble to come. Independence Day, July 1st arrived. All was quiet and the whole thing dismissed from our minds as a newspaper scare. However a few days after their public holiday ended, stories filtered through to Lusaka of terrible happenings. We approached the Red Cross and offered our services and accommodation in case of mass evacuation. That was on a Sunday morning; we heard nothing that day, but by the following evening cars were coming into Lusaka in increasing numbers. Voluntary organisations swung quickly into action; a reception centre was opened up; signs appeared in the street in French directing people on their way in from the north. On the Tuesday evening the radio programmes were interrupted every few minutes to give the latest news and instructions. It was like September 1939 all over again. Lusaka radio said that cars were pouring into the town. We made our way to the reception centre to enquire if help was needed. We were told that they had sufficient beds for the time being but needed guides to direct the refugees to the school hostels where arrangements had been made for the first batch of arrivals. We escorted some of them and went home to bed as no-one else was expected that night.

The following afternoon, after leaving the office, we reported once more to the reception centre and we were told that a large convoy was expected within an hour or so. We bought in extra food and stood by. As darkness fell it grew cold and windy and braziers were lit illuminating the silent groups of helpers. We heard the sound of approaching cars and witnessed the sad spectacle of women in flimsy dresses clutching their crying children, the men in bush shirts and shorts, as they had had no time to pack. Families had been separated, the old people sitting around looking lost and bewildered and all the time messages being relayed by loudspeakers in English and French trying to trace the lost ones. Some were fortunate and ran sobbing to their loved ones. It was a scene that I shall never forget.

After waiting for some time, we were allocated a young couple with a baby girl of two and a half months. They were given petrol coupons to see them through to Salisbury, a voucher for the car to be serviced and a packet of nappies for the baby. They were also given a box of cigarettes and a small amount of cash. Women from the WVS were busy sorting out warm clothing that had been quickly collected from the residents. The husband was a draughtsman with the Union Miniere Copper Mine and they had left everything except the carrycot and one suitcase to join a convoy of cars bound for Northern Rhodesia. Some of them had been stoned inside Northern Rhodesia territory, and the authorities were anxious to avoid further trouble, and the arrangement was for the refugees to stay for one night only and then travel south. Our guests spoke no English; they were bewildered and despondent and told us they could see no future anywhere. They would not be welcome in Belgium but there was nowhere else for them to go. As we sat discussing the general situation, I was disturbed to see the look of hatred in our cook's eyes. He had been with us for several years and had always been pleasant and friendly. I had made up the extra beds, attended to the meal and washed the dishes as it was late in the evening but he muttered "Too much work" and I realised that politics were behind this and I felt uneasy.

The following morning, I showed the young mother the kitchen, explained a few simple words of English in order that she could get milk for the baby as our sevants did not understand French. We then drove off to the garage, the young husband following. We wished him "Bon Voyage" and expected them to be on their way when we returned from work at lunch time. To our surprise as we drove back to the house, the young girl ran to the car. Tears streamed down her face as she called out *"Il est perdu."* Her husband had not returned. Her distress was understandable, alone in a strange country and we did our best to comfort her. We told her that he was probably still at the garage, and piling into the car, we drove quickly into town. Sure enough he was waiting for the repairs to the car. It had taken longer than expected. Her relief as she ran into his arms brought a lump to my throat.

The car was ready in the late afternoon. They planned to start immediately but mindful of the stoning and pointing out that darkness fell quickly and the nights were cold, we persuaded them to stay one more night. I wished we could have kept them longer to recover a little but we had stretched the rules and could do no more. That same evening, news came over the radio that the mine was opening up again and asking all employees to return. We explained this to our guests but he was most emphatic that he would never return. He said that all Africa was finished for the whites.

They set off the following morning. Things gradually quietened down; the streams of Congo cars slowly disappeared from the streets. Many Europeans decided to apply for permits for guns. Each application was considered on its merits depending on where they lived. Supplies of guns were exhausted in the shops and advertisements appeared in the newspapers saying that new stocks would be in shortly.

Meanwhile we were busy packing our household linen and effects to ship to England. As goods took a long time to reach the coast, we spent the last few weeks in a small hotel a few miles from town. This gave us a respite before the journey; no shopping or house to run, and no servant problems.

Just before we left the house, Sylvia was due to fly out for her summer holiday. The problem was, did we consider it safe for her to come out? We were all looking forward so much to being together again. Things seemed quiet and we let the arrangement stand. She flew out on the Comet and was thrilled to be with us again. Although we had been in Africa for almost thirteen years, we had seen no game and decided to have a holiday in the Wankie Game Reserve. The road was very bad but we felt it was worth making this last trip. We stayed in small huts just outside the entrance to the game reserve. They were simply furnished with comfortable beds. Cooking utensils were supplied and a boy was allocated to us for cooking and washing the dishes. The cooking was done on a fire outside. The meals were simple; mostly tinned stew and vegetables, as we took all our supplies with us. Each morning before breakfast we were booked out, the barrier raised, and we drove into the game reserve. This was the best time to see the animals. We saw buck of all kinds, zebras, giraffes, etc., all in their natural surroundings. We were warned never to get out of the car as it was too dangerous. Although there were about two thousand elephants in the reserve, we did not see any for a considerable time. Driving along the dirt track, we came upon a group of them in the distance by a small pool. We sat in the car and watched them as they splashed the muddy water over their bodies. We took cine shots with a telescopic lens and were most interested until several of them started moving towards the car. Sylvia was terrified and implored Daddy to drive away; one does not argue with elephants and we drove off. We searched for lions without success, until one morning we were driving across open grassland when we saw a number of cars at the side of the road. To our surprise people were standing beside their cars; a most foolish thing to do and strictly against the rules. They pointed out a number of lions, about fifteen of them, well away in the distance. They were too far away to photograph, but we did see lions after all. I liked the wart hogs; there were plenty of them always hurrying along like fussy housewives hurrying to do their shopping, reminding me of the Beatrix Potter books. The giraffes were difficult to see. It was surprising how they blended in with the trees; once we had seen them, we wondered how we could have missed them. During the middle of the day, there was nothing to be seen, and we usually rested and read a book in the shade or on the bed. At dusk we set out again as the animals went to the water holes. Taking photographs was not easy as there was no time to take a light reading; at the slightest sound they would bound away. On the return journey, we stayed a while at the Victoria Falls. How I loved that spot; it had always been my favourite place and I felt saddened as we gazed at that wonderful scene for the last time.

Sylvia's holiday came to an end all too soon, but this time as we saw her off at the airport it was not so hard to say goodbye. In a very short time we were to follow her. We had been in Lusaka over eleven years and had made many friends. We had a busy time going the rounds to say farewell. The African staff presented my husband with a pair of beautifully carved birds and two elephants. They told him they would cry when he went away; no unpleasantness there, only happy memories. We also had a very happy party with the European staff.

The day arrived for the final packing. We were awake at four o'clock and soon had the car loaded. It was raining heavily and to reach the car we had to step through thick mud. We laid newspapers on the floor but it was a muddy bedroom we left behind as we drove quietly away on our journey of two thousand miles. This time we did not linger sightseeing on the way. The weather improved as we neared the Cape. One of my last memories was of the peaches. Rows of cars were lined up by the roadside everyone offering trays of peaches for two shillings. It was pleasant to be in Cape Town once more. Driving up from the town, the view was breathtaking. The ships in the harbour looked like toy boats in a pool and all around were the mountains. We drove out to the Prime Minister's residence at Groote Schruer, a lovely Dutch-type house set in spacious grounds, that seemed to be one mass of hydrangeas of all shades.

On the last day of our stay in Cape Town, we were walking along Adderley Street, the traffic roaring along as usual, when glancing across the road I saw, to my horror, a coloured man, rolling over in the road; apparently he had been caught by a passing car. His girlfriend grabbed him and helped him across the road. This happened within a yard or two of the khaki-uniformed European policeman on traffic duty. He must have seen it but the traffic was not halted; the cars went dashing by, no-one took the slightest notice of the incident. I wondered if this type of incident was commonplace.

We went aboard the *Braemar Castle*; later we stood on deck as the ship's sirens sounded, watched the streamers being thrown from deck to dock and took our last look at Table Mountain as we sailed slowly out to sea and home to England.

As I look back on those days I remember the happy relationship we experienced with Africans as we trained them and passed on our skills, and the pleasant letter I received from my African clerk thanking me for the help I had given him in obtaining his promotion. The image of the gin-drinking European beating the Africans, did not exist where I lived. We were ordinary British families doing our job. I cannot believe that everything and everyone has changed — where did it all go wrong?